BRETHREN DRESS

A Testimony To Faith

by

Esther Fern Rupel

Published by the
BRETHREN ENCYCLOPEDIA, INC.
Philadelphia, Pennsylvania

1994

BRETHREN ENCYCLOPEDIA MONOGRAPH SERIES
William R. Eberly, editor
Number 5

BRETHREN DRESS
A TESTIMONY TO FAITH
Esther Fern Rupel

Copyright ©1994
Brethren Encyclopedia, Inc.

Availability of related materials: Related materials are available from The Brethren Encyclopedia, Inc.: *The Brethren Encyclopedia,* vols. I, II, and III (1983-1984); *The German Hymnody of the Brethren (1720-1903)* (1986); *Background and Development of Brethren Doctrines 1650-1987* (1989); *Brethren Beginnings/The Origin of the Church of the Brethren in Early Eighteenth Century Europe* (1992); *Hochmann von Hochenau 1670-1721* (1993); *The Complete Writings of Alexander Mack* (1991); and a paperback book entitled *Meet the Brethren* (1984). Requests for information or orders may be sent to The Brethren Encyclopedia, Inc., 313 Fairview Ave., Ambler, PA 19002.

Explanation of logo: The logo used on the title pages of the volumes of this series is derived from a seal which has been attributed to Alexander Mack, Jr. (1712-1803), son of the first Brethren minister and himself an active elder in colonial America. The *Brethren Encyclopedia* article on this "Mack seal" states, referring to the religious symbols: "Central to these is the cross, on which is superimposed a heart, suggesting a strong emphasis on sacrifice and devotion. The importance of bearing spiritual fruit is represented graphically by a vine, laden with grapes, whose branches spring from the heart. All of these symbols express an understanding of discipleship that was significant in the early history of the Brethren" (p. 775). The "Mack seal" has often been used by Brethren congregations on stationery, artwork, and publications.

ISBN 0-936693-50-9-X
Printed in the U.S.A.

TABLE OF CONTENTS

Chapter 5
CHURCH POLITY CONCERNING DRESS

Chapter 6
SUMMARY, CONCLUSIONS, AND RECOMMENDATIONS

LIST OF TABLES

LIST OF FIGURES

FOREWORD

One of the most distinctive and obvious characteristics of the Brethren (known as the German Baptist Brethren until 1908 when the name was changed to the Church of the Brethren) was their unique style of dress. This dress was prescribed and enforced by the Annual Conference, the highest legislative body of the Brethren. A prescribed dress is common among several small, Anabaptist groups (e.g., Amish) as well as some other religious bodies. In still other groups, prescribed dress is required for the clergy and special orders within the church, but not the general membership.

Among the Brethren, the Old German Baptist Brethren and the Dunkard Brethren require some form of prescribed dress. Some members of the Church of the Brethren wear some items of the earlier required dress, but most do not. The (Progressive) Brethren and the Grace Brethren have never legislated specific dress styles.

It is ironic that this most distinctive characteristic of the Brethren has never been the subject of articles or books by or about the Brethren. It is, therefore, significant that this present work by Esther Rupel is offered to readers interested in Brethren history, general religious life in America, history of clothing and costume, sociology of religion, and other related subjects.

One could hardly imagine a more qualified writer on the subject of Brethren dress than Esther Rupel. A life-long member of the Church of the Brethren, Dr. Rupel was born in Walkerton, Indiana, in 1924. After graduating from Manchester College in 1947 with a B.S. degree in home economics and art, she completed the vocational teaching license at Ball State University. She then taught home economics and art in the LaGrange Public Schools in Indiana for nine years, serving as a local 4-H leader most of this time.

A Master of Science degree in Home Economics was received from Purdue University in 1957 with a major in textiles and clothing. She then began a teaching career at Purdue University, West Lafayette, Indiana, as Professor of Clothing and Textiles in the department of Consumer Sciences and Retailing that spanned 31 years. During this time she completed a Ph. D. degree from the University of Minnesota in 1971. Her dissertation was entitled, "An Investigation of the Origin, Significance and Demise of the Prescribed Dress Worn by Members of the Church of the Brethren." The research for this dissertation is the basis for the present volume.

She is a life member of the American Home Economics Association, Indiana Home Economics Association, and Kappa Omicron Nu home economics honorary. She received the Best Teacher Award within the School of Home Economics at Purdue University and also received the General Foods Fund Fellowship for graduate study at the University of Minnesota. She was honored with an Outstanding Alumni Award by Manchester College in 1975. She has also served on the Board of Trustees of Manchester College. Since her retirement from Purdue University, Dr. Rupel is living at the Timbercrest Church of the Brethren Home in North Manchester, Indiana.

It is a major publishing event in the field of the Brethren history to present this work on Brethren Dress by Dr. Esther Fern Rupel.

William R. Eberly
Editor, Monograph Series
Brethren Encyclopedia, Inc.

PREFACE

The study of one's heritage honors the past, delineates its roots in the present, sets forth the values relevant for today, and clarifies a vision for the future. The genius of the Brethren is to relate religion to life, belief to practice, theology to ethics and to faithfully discharge these responsibilities as followers of Christ.

The purpose of this study was to investigate the origin, significance and demise of the mode of dress worn by members of the Church of the Brethren from its founding in Germany in 1708 to the present in America. The mode of dress, worn during the nineteenth and early part of the twentieth centuries has been given particular emphasis because it was prescribed for church membership. The mode differed from fashionable dress, symbolizing separation from the world. Conformity in dress was perceived as promoting unity of mind and spirit within the church membership. Changes in belief and of time and place brought changes in the mode and degree of conformity.

Of interest to students of costume and to many church members today is the issue of dress during a period of conformity. Even today members who were involved with the issues speak with emotion and desire that this story be made available for future generations. Others are curious as to why it came about, why it was held to so tenaciously, and what brought its demise. No single volume is available which portrays plain dress and speaks to the issues involved.

The aims of the study were: to prepare a concise record of the mode of dress worn by members of the Church of the Brethren, identify items of clothing with religious and social significance, note changes in items over time, and observe the extent that it is worn today. Also an attempt has been made to cite scriptural references and

beliefs which promoted the wearing of plain dress, its adoption and demise, and to analyze rulings passed by the governing body prescribing plain dress.

Historical study is seldom empirical in nature. The approach used for this study was a literature search and field work with findings reported in descriptive style. Resources available for study were: books on western European and American costume; church records, including minutes, histories, pamphlets, manuscripts, and photographs; family records, including histories, diaries, ledgers, letters, and photographs; extant examples of clothing; and informants who either wore or remembered plain dress. Throughout this volume, biblical references refer to the King James version of the Bible unless noted. The official minutes of Annual Meeting, along with the *Full Report,* available from years 1875 to 1930, and *The Brethren Encyclopedia* provided invaluable source material. *The Gospel Messenger* and other timely periodicals provided both individual and corporate opinions.

In the text, the terms "Brotherhood" and "Brethren" refer to the membership of the church as a whole, including both men and women. The term "brethren", without capitalization, refers to male members in general or a few in particular. Likewise, the term "sisters" refers to female members in general or in particular. The term "dress" is used throughout the text instead of "costume" in deference to those members who would have objected to the latter term because of its being indicative of a person portraying someone else by wearing a disguise. "Plain" dress refers to items of clothing worn for utilitarian purposes without ornamentation and ostentation, and especially those items required for membership in this socio-religious group. The word "testimony" is defined as a visual declaration of faith *via* clothing.

The term "sect" is used for a group seeking to establish the Kingdom of God on earth and separate from the world. Group members have in common a set of beliefs and values, homeland, language, and a mode of dress. Group bonds are strengthened by isolation, like occupations, endogamy and thus kinship. In time a simple and frugal lifestyle leads to economic success, permitting members to move to a higher socio-economic class, resulting in greater interaction with the world. With these changes, the group is no longer a sect but a church, and eventually changes its name.

Even before the thirteenth century, "sumptuary laws" were passed by both the medieval church and the crown for the purpose of controlling expenditure of the private purse for food, clothing, and entertainment, to keep subjects under control, maintaining the socio-economic class structure and preventing "moral decline". Although easily ignored, disobedience of these laws was to call forth the local governing officers and the wrath of Almighty God. Often these laws remain as relics on statute books long after economic and social forces brought relaxation of their enforcement and shifts in human behavior.

Years of reading and teaching in the area of western European and American costume were drawn on by the author for this manuscript. However, she was dependent on the work of other authors regarding reasons for wearing clothing and bodily adornment, and for insights regarding conforming and deviant behavior within a socio-cultural group and presentation of clothing cues by cultural groups.

This study was limited by scarcity of information regarding dress from 1708 to 1830. Lack of extant examples is due to clothing items being worn out, passed to other family members, used for burial, or cut up for domestic purposes. In-formation is limited to outer garments having religious significance and worn to church and social occasions. Daily wear differed very little in style, and undergarments had no significance other than propriety. Children's clothing has been deleted because infant baptism is not practiced, and the prescribed dress was adopted by the adult applicant upon affirmation of faith at baptism. Many scattered sources of information housed with local churches and individuals across the Brotherhood were not available because copies have yet to be deposited in historical collections at Brethren colleges or archives. Pictorial illustrations and photographs were prohibited as late as 1904. Those available were often wedding portraits taken in photographic studios. The photographic skills of the author were tested when copying illustrations on locale and catching the image of black and white items with clarity on the same negative.

A brief history of the Church of the Brethren, formerly called German Baptist Brethren, has been included for the benefit of the reader unacquainted with the church's history. Many other excellent historical resources are listed throughout the bibliography.

The Brethren were sincere in their beliefs and attempted to apply them to daily living. The scriptures were searched repeatedly to find answers to problems. They were open to new revelations by the Holy Spirit. The polity of the church, being democratic, allowed for discussions about plain dress, although it was a secondary issue to more major issues as scriptural interpretation, observance of the ordinances, and spreading God's saving grace to a lost world.

The topic under discussion has touched the author in several ways: a professional career teaching historic textiles and costume, the care of extant examples of plain dress left to her keeping (or demise), and observance of the phenomenon at church. She was reared in a Brethren family with a rich tradition and a deep commitment to the church. At the age of twelve she was baptized to membership in the Pine Creek Church of the Brethren in Northern Indiana District and adopted the cap. The reading of minutes and manuscripts and conversations with others in regard to the issue of wearing plain dress has challenged her to review the tenets of her faith and to examine her lifestyle as a testimony of her belief. She asks that the reader forgive any lack of clarity, inaccuraries, omissions and misinterpretations in her preparation of this volume.

Acknowledgment and appreciation must be expressed to Dr. Gertrude Esteros and Dr. Suzanne Davison at the University of Minnesota for their encouragement during academic studies and for supervision of the initial research on this topic. Findings were compiled as a doctoral dissertation, entitled "An Investigation of the Origin, Significance and Demise of the Prescribed Dress Worn by Members of the Church of the Brethren", University of Minnesota, 1971. Gratitude is also extended for the untiring efforts of librarians and their assistants for locating and free use of source materials at: Brethren Historical Library and Archives, Church of the Brethren General Offices, Elgin, Illinois; Zug Memorial Library, Elizabethtown College, Elizabethtown, Pennsylvania; Beeghley Library, Juniata College, Huntingdon, Pennsylvania; Funderburg Library, Manchester College, North Manchester, Indiana; and First Church of the Brethren, Philadelphia, Pennsylvania. Appreciation is expressed to the Annual Conference manager permitting a display of photographs at the 183rd Annual Conference, Louisville, Kentucky.

The author is most appreciative of the assistance of over two hundred members and friends of the church interested in this study and their cordiality as hosts. They generously shared their time and energies by searching through bookshelf and trunk to supply resource materials and extant examples of clothing they cherished dearly to answer my many questions during personal interviews and by personal letters in order that information on Brethren dress might be recorded for posterity. Finally, sincere gratitude is expressed to my mother, Edith Rohrer Rupel, for her continued encouragement, and to my sister, Annabel J. Rupel, for her valuable assistance and critical reading of the manuscript.

Esther Fern Rupel
North Manchester, Indiana
June, 1994

This volume is dedicated to those
brothers and sisters who wore plain
dress with integrity and purpose.

Chapter 1

INTRODUCTION

Costume is not static, but responds to the forces of the social milieu and portrays the time and place of which it is a part. Man has the capability to abstract from the fabric of daily life its color, its pulsating rhythms, its victories and its defeats and then in turn to weave these attributes of life into the clothing that he wears. The genius with which this is done has continued to cause the student of costume to marvel.

By studying the historic costumes of a cultural group, the sensitive student is able to partially recreate the past life of the group. Despite difficulties in gathering adequate data and errors of deletion, addition, and misemphasis in reconstructing the patterned maze of history from the remnants at hand, the behavioral patterns of the cultural group become clearer. By juggling these ravellings from the past, the investigator is able to order the sequence of events, to feel the moods of the characters, to look at the goals of their purposeful endeavor, to uncover their answers to problems, and to perceive factors resulting in cultural change. What at first seems almost beyond the bounds of comprehension becomes more distinct as the woof of place is inserted into the warp of time. The purpose is not to cut away a part or to apply a patch of camouflage, but to rinse out the dust formed from more recent pursuits that the threads of past virtues might be extricated from the noils of human frailty. The student whose hand has become sensitive to the textures of fur and fabric and whose eye can grasp the temperament of line and devotion to detail perceives costumes as works of art. The insights gained culminate in an acceptance of the person who wore it and an appreciation for the values he held.

Costumes of the past portray that which was present for their time and place. They are not repeated in their totality because the forces of time and the conditions of place do not return. By relating to the past, one recognizes forces which have culminated in the present as to who one is and what one does in regard to dress. With the passage of time the dress of this day will vividly portray for future students of historic costume the tapestry of life which is being woven.

The Problem

This study is an investigation of the origin, significance, and demise of the mode of dress worn by members of the Church of the Brethren, from its founding in Germany in 1708 to 1970 in America. Emphasis is placed on the mode of dress prescribed for church membership during the nineteenth century and early part of the twentieth century. During this time considerable conformity developed in the dress of both men and women. Attempts to symbolize separation from the world, to create greater unity within the church, and to retain the mode of dress which developed, resulted in many rules regarding dress being passed by the highest authoritative body of the church. Although the majority of the membership in 1970 no longer adhered to the prescribed dress, a few members continued to dress in this manner.

The mode of dress of the members of the Church of the Brethren differed from that worn by society in general and is of particular interest to the student of costume and to members of the church focusing attention on their heritage. To date there has not been compiled a concise record dealing with the dress of this religious group. Only smatterings about their costume appear in historic costume books in general. Source materials have remained scattered. The historian, the dramatist, the illustrator and the publisher dealing with the history of this religious group have had no guide for use in their work.

During discussions on this topic members of the church expressed much interest. Elderly members who were involved with the issue speak with emotion. Younger members have only a scant notion of the conditions of its occurrence. Many members willingly shared information, photographs, and items of clothing that the history of this phenomenon within the life of the church might be preserved for posterity.

Objectives

It is the purpose of this study:

1. to provide a concise record of the mode of dress worn by members of the Church of the Brethren to be used as a guide by the church historian, dramatist, illustrator, and publisher;

2. to identify the items of clothing worn by members of the church which had religious and social significance;

3. to note changes in the prescribed items of clothing;

4. to observe the extent that the prescribed dress was worn in 1970;

5. to analyze rulings regarding dress in the official minutes of business meetings held at the local, district, and particularly at the national level; and

6. to point out beliefs which promoted conformity in dress, the adoption of a prescribed

mode of dress, and its demise.

Resources Available

Five types of resources were used in the investigation and documentation of the clothing issue:

1. books and costume collections concerning western world costume in general;

2. church records consisting of official minutes of business meetings, books on church history, pamphlets, tracts, periodicals, recorded addresses, and photographs;

3. family records consisting of family histories, ledgers, letters, diaries, and photographs;

4. items of clothing worn by a member of the church, with examination and notation made of cut, color, type of fabric, and construction detail; and

5. knowledgeable persons who provided information through personal interviews and correspondence.

Limitations

Reconstructing the historic past always has been liable to the inadequacies of data, the misinterpretations of available data, and lack of proper emphasis on the part of both authors and investigators. Only recently members of the church have taken an interest in the history of their church. These factors have made for limitations specific to this study.

1. This study was limited to the mode of dress worn by members of the Church of the Brethren, formerly known as the conservative branch of the German Baptist Brethren. The investigation has not dealt with the dress of other groups of the same origin which separated from this main church body.

2. Discussion has been limited to outer garments worn for dress occasions by adult members. Outer garments were visible symbols signifying membership in this socio-religious group. Clothing worn for daily wear had less religious significance and underclothing had none beyond

that of propriety. Prior to the twentieth century individuals seeking membership were young adults; therefore, discussion concerning children's clothing was deleted.

3. A scarcity of records made for minimal information concerning the dress worn during the first one and one-half centuries of the history of the church, 1708-1858.

4. Library collections on the history of the church located at the six church related colleges, the seminary, and the publishing house have received preliminary organization, with much remaining to be done.

5. The minutes for the Annual Meetings held before 1778 were not preserved. Those available were found to be consecutive only from 1830 to 1970. It was impossible to peruse the available historical records of local churches and district meetings since these records remain widely scattered across many states.

6. Many periodicals were published as individual enterprises and thus were short lived. Some copies were at hand, but complete bound volumes were lacking. Furthermore, these periodicals have not been indexed. Information had to be gleaned by turning individual pages. Some were in the format of a large newspaper, making the duplication of extensive articles for further study almost prohibitive in cost.

7. The German language was used extensively by members of the church until the middle of the nineteenth century. Some members were able to read and write only a little German and no English. Hand written letters in German script were almost impossible to decipher. The German newspapers published by Christopher Sauer in Colonial America have not been translated, although they have been microfilmed.

8. The number of items of clothing for this study was limited for several reasons. The best clothing was used for burial garments in place of a shroud. The second best clothing was given to another member in the family or in the church. Badly worn clothing was used for making bedding, rag carpets, or cleaning cloths. Unsuccessful attempts used to restore some items destroyed them. A lack of appreciation or of knowledge as to their value caused many items to be thrown away. As large family homesteads gave way to smaller houses, little space was allowed for storing relics.

9. Pictorial illustrations were scarce because Protestantism rejected the use of religious art forms in worship. Furthermore, the early Brethren were opposed to portrait paintings and photographs because they perceived them to be graven images fostering idolatry. Before 1904 taking photographs was in disregard to the rules of the church. Some of the photographs located were of insufficient quality for reproduction. Wedding portraits were the most numerous of any type found, sometimes showing only a partial view of the figures in a studio setting. No photographs were found showing the back view of a garment, and only a very few showing a side view. Only a few photographs were found showing outer wraps and everyday apparel, all of which were taken in the twentieth century. Because of a lack of appropriate settings, models and accessory items, it was necessary to photograph available items of clothing on dress forms in an artificial setting. Since a professional photographer was not readily available at all times, it became necessary to use the photographic skills of the author.

10. Finally, the items of clothing overlapped as to the periods of time worn and as to the locations in which they were worn. This overlapping complicated the sequencing and dating of available items of clothing.

Chapter 2

HISTORICAL REVIEW

Although clothing has been considered a primary need of mankind, only in the twentieth century has it been the subject of serious study. Emphasis has shifted from the problems of production and consumption and from its aesthetic attributes to its effect on human behavior. Since World War II researchers have begun to explore the sociological and psychological implications of clothing, and, since 1960, its cultural aspects from an anthropological point of view. (26:vii)

The study of the clothing worn by this particular socio-religious group provides an historical example of the clothing behavior of a subcultural group. Theories regarding man's motives for wearing clothing aid in the understanding of the clothing behavior of individual members of a group. The symbolic interaction theory of social psychology furthers understanding of why a particular mode of dress was developed by the subcultural group, why it held meaning for the group, and why it met demise. Items of clothing used by any cultural group are seldom found to be without historical precedent in use and symbolic meaning.

The social structure of a subcultural group is composed of a hierarchy of statuses. The group prescribes the behavior of the members fulfilling the accompanying roles. The degree of restriction placed upon the items of clothing and the manner in which they are worn reflects the degree of restriction placed upon the role by the group. The usurping of clothing belonging to upper class members by lower class members is perceived as disruptive to the social organizational structure. Therefore those in authority combat the threat to their present status by passing rules, or sumptuary laws, to regulate the dress and maintain the social structure.

This particular subcultural group was held together by a commonality of daily problems of living, ethnic origin, and religious beliefs. In their search for religious truth, the charter members adopted beliefs which led to the organization of a religious sect in opposition to the institutionalized church of their day. A study of the history of this religious group shows that, as they attempted to maintain this separation and to apply their beliefs to everyday living, the manner of clothing the physical body became an issue of the membership.

Theories Regarding Clothing

The wearing of clothing is a human characteristic. The reasons why man wears clothing seem relatively simple on first consideration. Further study reveals how elusive have been the real answers. Reasons propounded by an individual are satisfactory to him, although they may be lacking in logic. Arguments supporting the wearing of clothing are quickly refuted by evidence, differing interpretation, drawn from another cultural group.

Motives for the wearing of clothing, thought to be universal in nature, have been grouped under five basic themes: for bodily comfort, for modesty, for aesthetic expression, for expression of the self, and for signifying social status. (26:12) Clothing does contribute to the comfort of the human body, unable to adjust to extreme fluctuations in temperature, or to shield itself from the sting of insects, blowing sand, or projectiles thrown by other men. By the insertion of pockets into clothing to carry objects, the hands are free for other activities.

A sense of modesty has not been perceived as an innate human characteristic but a result of habitually having clothed the body. Seldom in history has complete nudity received social approval. Nakedness has been considered immoral by some cultural groups but not by others. In cultures influenced by the Judeo-Christian religion, nakedness was believed to be a causative factor of sin. It was claimed that covering the body permitted the mind to focus attention on spiritual matters. Therefore clothing was perceived as a tool for maintaining the moral code in western European civilizations. (26:61) A logical conclusion from this mode of thought is that the greater the area of the body that is clothed, the higher the moral standard of the wearer. This argument is quickly refuted when the body form is revealed by tight clothing, or when clothing is used to attract attention to the body.

Bodily adornment can not be classified as either primitive or civilized for it is practiced by both groups. It is a response to the basic human need for favorable responses on the part of one's associates. Cosmetics, jewelry, and clothing are used to give expression to the self and to increase the stimulating effect of one person upon another. Physical adornment has been frowned upon by religious groups for at least three reasons. Alteration of the physical form is meddling with what God has created as perfect. Time and resources should be expended in more gainful activity. Adornment incites physical passions, restricting those of a spiritual nature. These activities are at variance with beliefs which hold spirituality above carnality. Pride in personal appearance is considered false pride.

Clothing communicates symbolically the social position or status of a person to others. In brief, it denotes age, sex, socio-economic class, occupation, marital status, and membership in a cultural group. The various attributes of a costume provide further cues. The cut, the color, the quality, the condition, and the manner in which an item is worn makes for even more subtle distinctions. Numerous changes of raiment display the extent of a person's wealth. The presence of an item communicates status and also its absence. Ceremonial clothing is also considered a requisite for the worship of a supreme deity. (24:251)

Symbolic Interaction Theory

The symbolic interaction theory of social psychology appears relevant in explaining the clothing behavior of social groups. Man's environment is both physical and symbolic. Symbols have been defined as the residue of social interaction. (42:5) They consist of: physical forms, such as an object or a person; movements, such as a gesture or activity; or an idea. They often appear in clusters, rather than in isolation. Forms take on symbolic meaning when they have been a part of a significant experience for a person or a group. Consensus as to their meaning is established through group interaction.

The symbolic behavior of man is learned, accumulated, integrated, and evaluated through human interaction. The meanings of symbols are conditioned by both individual and subcultural goals. The value of objects and other physical forms above their intrinsic worth is in terms of the ends of the individual and the cultural group. Two goals basic to any subcultural group are the living of the "good life" by each individual and the perpetuation of the group as a whole. (10:274) Some symbols have greater significance than others in the attainment of these goals. The individual group member and the group as a whole arrange symbols in hierarchies.

Instrumental acts taken in regard to symbols significant to the group are subject to the social norms of the group. (52:441) The meanings of symbols change with the passage of time both for an individual and for the subcultural group. As symbols are transferred to the next generation, their preservation becomes the heritage of the group while their use becomes the foundation of everyday living and future progress. (42:16)

Society in general and a subcultural group in particular delimit the broad range of symbols developed by man and the broad range of responses within man's capability. A person makes a rapid summation of clothing cues or symbols presented before making a response. Whether he draws correct or incorrect inferences about the symbols presented is dependent upon his perception and his knowledge of the meaning of the forms reviewed. His response is then subject to validation by other persons. A correct summation of the cues presented leads to further interaction. Errors in summation cause him to make errors in communication which lead to embarrassment and to interruption of the interaction process. (26:109) Both the presence and the absence of a significant symbol affects behavior.

Symbolic Meaning of Clothing

History has recorded the fact that many items of clothing have carried both social and religious significance. However, the reason an item was endowed with a particular meaning has been lost over time and is left to conjecture. Briefly, a man's hair style, hat, glove, cravat, coat, shirt, trousers, belt or girdle, and shoes all denote social status with regard to sex, age, social class, and ethnic background. (24:245) The garments of a woman denote social status for her also. The removal of any one item voluntarily or by force denotes a loss of status.

The headdress is considered the most symbolic part of an individual's costume. (24:245)

The hair and beard of a man is perceived as denoting manliness, virility, age, and experience. Also, it is associated with holding membership in some social and religious organizations. To remove the hair or beard denotes the loss of the above attributes. A voluntary removal of the hat on the part of a man denotes deference to a person of higher rank. A cleric bares his head as the vicar of Christ. (11:31) Refusal to remove one's hat signifies the wearer's failure to recognize differences in rank. Refusal to remove one's hat in deference to other men for religious reasons implies that social rank is an invention of man and only God is to be recognized as having a higher status.

In the past a woman did not remove her hat or glove in deference to men because she was not of equal rank. To have done so would have suggested rivalry. The cap or coif, adopted by a woman of Western Europe at the time of her marriage, signified subjection to her husband. (204) Hats, hoods, and bonnets were worn over the cap. The type of these headdresses varied with the status of the wearer and the period of history. These items had less religious significance than the veil.

Other items of clothing also had social significance. An apron was worn for protection of other clothing while performing menial tasks. Therefore it became a symbol of servitude and still is worn by the servant class. A man wears his apron only during the hours he is performing vocational tasks, whereas a woman wears hers continually. The official aprons of the bishop, the dean, and Freemason imply that they are servants of the people. In the past the wearing of shoes symbolized a free man, for the slave had none. The kissing of the shoe by another person implied complete subservience. A kerchief was used in various ways as a cover for the head, the neck, the chest, or was carried in the hand. (30:675) Horn suggests that the cravat is the single index of a man's status at the present time. (26:163)

The social roles of the ancient Hebrews were rigidly defined within the cultural group. The exchange of clothing between the sexes was forbidden by Hebraic law, Deuteronomy 22:5. Transvestitism was considered sin and subjected the wearer to the legal code. Until recently, in countries influenced by European cultures, a bifurcated garment denoted its wearer as a man, and a skirt denoted its wearer as a woman. An imposter was a "wolf in sheep's clothing" seeking the reward without the responsibilities of an office. A person invested with the garb of an office is expected to render the appropriate service in order to receive his just rewards.

The investiture of new clothing at baptism has significance. This occasion symbolizes the burial of one's past life and the beginning of a new manner of living. Clothing is perceived as a requisite for fulfilling one's role as a religious officiant. The church has had an order of dress for the office of the priesthood and its subsidiary offices for many centuries. Vestments are used to invoke the appropriate feelings and behavior and thus deter the inappropriate in both the wearer and the observer. (51:92) The absence of an item is perceived as invoking the displeasure of the deity and its presence as worthy of granting a blessing.

The continued use of priestly robes generated in the minds of the laity a belief that they were sacred. Catholicism has retained the use of vestments for its clergy during the celebration of the mass. In recent years there has been a trend away from elaborate chasubles in favor of more simple styles. Protestantism rejected elaborate priestly robes and adopted black gowns with a white accent at the neck. This white cloth was a vestige of the amice which protected the chasuble from soil. More recently the standing collar has become indicative of a cleric, and the shirt collar fulfills the function of the amice. (8:61)

Protestant religious groups consider Christ to be their vicar who makes conciliation for them with the Father God. Appellation is then possible without further human intervention. Some religious groups believe that at baptism all applicants become ordained ministers or servants of the Most High. (174:16) Since all members are of equal rank, there is little difference between the dress of the officiant and the lay member.

The Subcultural Group

Research has shown that a subcultural group develops within a larger society when members interact significantly more with each other than they do with other members in society. (17:291) The boundaries of a subcultural area are not set directly by geographical lines or by formal group membership, but by limits of effective communication. (48:136) Communication is greater among persons who hold similar interests and values than those holding dissimilar ones.

When the interaction of individual persons continues over a period of time, the characteristics of a social group appear. The membership is established, and members are aware of who is and who is not one of the group. Conversation follows along certain topics. Task differentiation results in a structured system of statuses and roles, including those of leader and follower. A system of values and beliefs and a code of ethics regarding proper attitudes and behavior develops, and ranges of acceptable behavior are set. Each member becomes aware of a feeling of belongingness, of obligations, and of mutual support. (10:274) A subcultural group remains a separate entity if it is a self-contained economic unit; if its government is autonomous; if its values, ideologies, and social habits are a continuation of the past; and if religion and daily life are integrated. (29:409)

Status has been defined as one's place in his social group. (58:250) Some statuses are regarded as more desirable than others. The extent of the rights and privileges granted by a social group to an individual is in regard to his status. Clothing is regarded as the ever present symbol of status. The social group prescribes what clothing is appropriate for each status.

Each person has more than one status, which is either ascribed or achieved. One's status with regard to sex, age, ethnic group, and individual talents is ascribed at birth. On occasion wealth, occupation, and powers of supernaturalism are ascribed also. The behavior which accompanies an ascribed status is learned after the status is granted by the social group. The mode of dress for a given status is adopted when the status is granted, and the manner of wearing it is then learned. Statuses with regard to occupational skills, marriage, leadership, or wealth, attained by effort on the part of the individual, are designated as achieved. The appropriate behavior is learned before the status is granted by the social group. (24:386) Investiture with the proper attire is then a part of the celebration of such achievements. Since an achieved status is acquired, a disrobing is necessary if the status is lost.

Changes in age, health, occupation, wealth, education, or affiliation force or permit an individual to change his status. In turn a change in status forces or permits an individual to change his mode of dress. When a person changes from one status in life to another, he often experiences feelings of anxiety because of the uncertainty of the behavior that is expected. Much thought and preparation is given to ceremonial clothing for such an occasion. Practice makes for an assured performance at the ceremony or initiation rite before a gathering of kin and friends. (26:142) Finally the new status is announced by using the appropriate titles and by granting new privileges and responsibilities.

A social role has been defined as the behavior associated with a given status within a social group. (51:93) Usually a highly restrictive role is accompanied by an explicit mode of dress.

(26:137) A lack of role definition on the part of the social group makes for a wide variation in the clothing worn. (26:144) Regardless of the degree of restriction, a model of the clothing to be worn by an individual member when fulfilling a role is furnished by the group.

Fulfilling all aspects of the behavior required by a new status is a concern of the novice. The possibility always exists that there remains evidence of behavior identified with the previous status. Therefore efforts may be overdone to fulfill every minute detail of the prescribed behavior. Means for obtaining the model clothing may be provided by the group. Often new initiates receive free the required items of dress during initiation rites.

Imitating those who have already assumed the role is a means of learning the appropriate clothing behavior and results in a person receiving positive sanctions. The group which granted the new status validates an individual's behavior by the granting of additional rights and privileges. Should behavior meet disapproval, the rights and privileges are withheld which causes anxiety on the part of the individual. (58:254)

Individuals have more than one status within a cultural group, and thus play more than one role. These statuses, and in turn the corresponding roles, implement each other if compatible. Compatibility depends in part on whether the statuses are based on the same or similar values, and demand the same or similar behavior. Then clothing selected to assist a person in fulfilling one role often assists in fulfilling the other.

A person is capable of interacting with more than one person in a significant manner. These persons become his reference group. Significant social interaction results in a code for behavior, including the mode of dress required for group membership. A reference group has two functions in regard to the individual, comparative and normative. (28:355) An individual as a member of the group not only shares his fate with his reference group but also compares his fate with others in the group. Happiness with regard to clothing is perceived in terms of having what others in the group have. Unhappiness is perceived as deprivation. The normative function of a reference group is to determine what are "right" and "good" attitudes and behavior for the group and for its individual members, and what are "wrong" or "bad" attitudes and behavior, including behavior in regard to clothing.

Conformity and deviation are considered to be opposing aspects of the same phenomenon in human behavior. Conformity in dress is defined as following a previously established pattern of action, in this case designated by the social group. Deviation in dress is defined as an irregularity in the pattern previously established, thus disvalued by the social group. (7:148) The adoption of a uniform implies the willingness of a person to give up personal rights to act independently in order to conform to the specifications laid down by the social group. (26:144) If the individual was involved in drawing up the dress code, he is aware why the rules were made. Commitment to the basic beliefs held by the group makes for conformity in behavior because the rules have meaning. If the beliefs of the group have not been internalized, the behavior of a person is either perfunctory or irregular.

The solidarity of a group is dependent upon adherence to its norms by individual members. A group in tension is sustained by either tightening its controls or redefining its norms. (7:153) Tangible signs of group membership are most significant during periods of rivalry with other groups. Sherif found in studying adolescent group behavior that one of the narrowest ranges of individual behavior with regard to group participation pertained to clothing. (47:170) Inconsistency in rules often forms a large part of the argument favoring deviant behavior. If enough members defect, the group disintegrates. Defection takes place when the interaction is

no longer satisfying to the members and when the organization becomes an obstacle rather than an instrument for pursuing the essentials of daily living. Shifts in the values and beliefs may be made by a group to maintain its membership. Unless a group permits change, it clings to the past remnants of its ideology until exhaustion brings about its demise. (7:153)

Sumptuary Laws

The behavior found within a cultural group has been classified as being governed by one of four types of social control. (26:55) Behavior labelled a "folkway" is the generally accepted or popular way of doing something at a given time. Such a practice is relatively widespread throughout the interacting group. A person failing to conform is not confronted with criticism or more severe measures of discipline. Often failure is dismissed as a personal idiosyncracy. Behavior deviating from a folkway regarding dress is permitted because it is perceived as causing no harm to the group's way of living or continuance.

In contrast to folkways, "customs" prevail for longer periods of time, usually for more than one generation. The social pressure for conforming to a customary mode of dress is considerably greater than for a folkway. "Mores" with regard to clothing concern behavior which bear moral or ethical connotations as to whether the behavior is "right" or "wrong". Action is taken by members of a group to enforce clothing standards which are perceived as morally right. Nonconforming repetitive behavior results in the passage of explicit rules or laws regarding clothing. Laws have two functions: the designation of misdemeanors and the designation of an authority to enforce punishment. (24:482) Punishment is inflicted with the intent of diverting further misdemeanors on the part of the deviant or group member. The purpose of retribution and rehabilitation is to restore the deviant individual to his former status within the group.

Sumptuary laws are passed to protect an individual's status and to maintain the social, political, and moral order of the state. Explicitly they are passed to control the private expenditure of the individual purse for food, clothing, entertainment, and personal habits. In addition they are considered to be a means of maintaining social class distinction and to prevent moral decline induced by high living. (53:464)

A characteristic of a static society is that a distinction exists between members of the various social classes. The clothing of the next higher socio-economic class often is attainable with only a minimal expenditure of material resources available to the lower class through a change in the basic economic situation of the country. Thus it is possible for a person to appear as belonging to the next higher status even though he may not have reached it in other respects. The adoption of the dress of the higher social class by the lower social class is considered to be disruptive of the social structure. (53:464) In the past sumptuary laws were used to regulate the kind of fabric or fur, the color, the cut, and the decorative details of clothing. Restrictions were placed on the kind and amount of lace, passementerie, and gems which could be used on garments worn even in the hierarchy of court circles. (53:465) A display of extravagance was considered to be displeasing to God and ruinous to the individual. The expenditure of wealth on affluent living was believed to be basis of moral decline. These laws were further supported by the belief that God punished mankind for these sins. Punishment was brought upon an individual and upon a nation in the form of scourges of plague, fire, earthquakes, and war.

Sumptuary laws were found extensively in all the countries of Western Europe from the thirteenth to the nineteenth centuries. The church, being under the hand of the state, perceived the loss of status by royalty as a threat to herself.

Thus she upheld the edicts of the crown, published those of her own, and called forth the vengeance of the Almighty against offenders. (53:466)

Sumptuary laws often are blatantly disobeyed on the part of the wearer, circumvented by connivance, or ignored. The enforcement of these laws is most difficult because the extravagancies which they attempt to control are a result of changes in the basic economy. (53:464) Furthermore the wide variation as to content and their method of enforcement makes for inconsistencies. Arrests are dependent upon the personal judgment of the arresting officer. Observation shows that a period of high activity on the part of prosecuting officers is followed by a lull. Often the problem is solved by a change in fashionable attire. However, sumptuary laws remain on statute books as vestiges of attempts to retain class distinctions of a former day. (53:466)

The Christian Church and Sects

Christians believe that the church was established by divine authority. Members of sects hold the same belief. The differences between a religious sect and a church is a matter of polarities. For the most part practices which the one accepts, the other rejects.

The duty of the **church** is perceived as the sanctification of the world by providing a channel between God and man. The world is in it, and it is in the world. All persons within the boundaries of the community are its wards. The children of believers are accepted as members by infant baptism. Thus the conversion experience is not a spectacular event, but rather a gradual process. The sacraments are served to both the member and nonmember. The beliefs spelled out are more encompassing than those of a sect. Salvation is assured by faith. The responsibility of disciplining one's daily living is a matter of conscience. The governing processes are not necessarily democratic. The leadership is trained to assume its place in the ecclesiastical hierarchy. By having aligned it-self with society, the church is subjected to fur-ther compromises and accommodations. Vari-ous ventures of the church are performed with the assistance of the state. Its missionary ac-tivities are formalized and weak. In time small groups are formed in protest to the aloofness, formality, and institutionalism which develop. (40:130)

The duty of a **sect** is perceived as the estab-lishment of the kingdom of God on earth by separating itself physically from society at large. Although membership is voluntary, a conver-sion experience is a requirement for joining the group. The vows of commitment are addressed to a well defined set of beliefs. Proper conduct is considered of utmost importance for the insurance of salvation and is enforced by a strict discipline. Government is democratic with lay personnel providing the leadership. Emphases are placed upon the separation of the church from the state, the converted from the uncon-verted, and the future world from the present. Attempts by a sect to return to the style of life of the first century apostolic church are to bypass the institutionalism which has developed in the church over time. Because the world is perceived as a source of new converts, the missionary spirit abounds with little delay due to formalities. A sect usually lasts only one generation unless it becomes an "established sect" or an adjunct arm of the church. (40:131)

Sects have many beliefs in common, but when compared, differences are evident. O'Dea clas-sified sects into four types, with the third type pertinent to this study. A sect which withdraws from society to cultivate inner spirituality was called "introversionist". (40:134) Included in this type were the German Pietists of the seventeenth and eighteenth centuries. Although they did not form a formal organization, they affected the beliefs of other sectarian groups that did. They aroused a sense of personal worth and dignity within the individual, taught self-discipline, fur-

thered humanitarian reform, and in America sup-ported the proponents of democracy. (39:628)

Observation has shown that the development of sects is a lower class phenomenon. Often their membership is drawn from a people who have been disinherited from their land or other eco-nomic resources and uprooted from their social moorings by events beyond their control. Thrown together by fate, interaction soon joins together those with like interests. In time a charismatic leader develops from within the group. (40:132) The functions performed by a sect for the in-dividual member have been noted as complex. It provides an outlet for strain and frustration resulting from a member's position in society. The situation is reconciled further by the ad-dition of new meanings and a set of values for the reorganization of the member's personal life. Often ways are developed which provide for economic and social needs. Physical needs are cared for from the resources within the group, sometimes held in common. (40:132)

A sect becomes "established" by withdrawal from the world. Therefore it relinquishes its mili-tant spirit to change the world for a more pacifistic one. By establishing a separate com-munity, only minimal dependence is made upon the larger society, but greater dependence is made on the group. Interaction within the group is promoted by a commonality of values and beliefs, similarity of problems, often a common homeland, thus a common language, and mode of dress. With the passage of time endogamy is practiced, strengthening group bonds through kinship. A similarity in pursuits of labor, often agricultural, aids isolation by natural geographic boundaries. (39:627)

The life of simplicity and frugality observed by members of a sect results in some measure of economic success. It then becomes possible for members to assume a higher class status in an open class society. (40:131) This new po-sition furthers interaction with the world and brings about worldly expectations and accommodations to it. The members are able to establish a new identity. They now have a place in the world, accept it, and take on its ways. Changes within the religious practices of a sect are blamed on the relaxation of restrictions by succeeding generations; variance in practices in different locales; training of the clergy; shifts in ideas due to forceful discussions resulting from schisms; and increased contacts with the larger society. (39:627) However, changes in the overall society, such as increased physical mobility, urbanization, improved economic conditions and industrialization, have even greater bearing upon a sect. The extent is commensurate with its interaction with society at large. (40:132) As a result of these forces, a group loses its sectarian characteristics and takes on those of a church, often signified by changing its name.

The use of disciplinary measures by a religious group has as its purpose the reclamation of the individual and the purification of the church. It is a means of maintaining order which in turn strengthens and preserves the solidarity of the religious group. Punishment consists of penance, avoidance, and excommunication, the latter two used particularly by religious sects.

Exclusion from a religious community carries three degrees of punishment: loss of office, exclusion from participation in communion service, and complete banishment with or without opportunity for restoration. (21:673) Social isolation of the deviant encourages conformity in behavior among group members. Furthermore, it slows down social change by preventing the injection of new ideas or forms of behavior. (25:349) Avoidance and excommunication serve as a deterent to unacceptable behavior because of the fear of disassociation, suspension of rights, and commitment to eternal perdition.

Sectarianism has been considered an evil by the Christian church, a signal of its disintegration. Niebuhr did not take this position. (39:360) He felt that sects were creative religious movements. By their reoccurrence the church has been forced to take a look at itself and to initiate reforms to overcome its accommodation to the conditions in the world. In particular, the insistance by sects that religion is a matter of individual conviction and the insistance of the maintenance of a code of ethics counterbalances the collective authority and dogma of the church.

Chapter 3

A BRIEF HISTORY OF THE CHURCH OF THE BRETHREN

A religious sect pushes forward in the purposes expressed in its beliefs, but its course is subject to the conditions of time and place of which it is a part. The origin of the Church of the Brethren in Europe and the influence of other groups is diagrammatically expressed in Figure 1. The transplantation to America, the divisions within the membership, and the names designating each group are given in the diagram.

This discussion on Brethren history is divided into three parts: the period in Europe from 1708 to 1733, the period in America from 1719 to 1800, and from 1801 to 1970. Discussion is limited to a brief glimpse of the cultural setting, significant activities, and organizational structure of the church acting as an authoritative body. The beliefs held by the Brethren at the origin of the church are stated, and a further interpretation is given for 1970. A review of other sources on Brethren history is necessary to feel the rhythms of daily living and to see the color in the pageantry of human events in the lives of the Brethren.

Europe, 1708-1733

Germany as the seat of the Protestant Reformation continued to spawn new groups with religious fervor. Under the direction of Alexander Mack, Sr., eight persons who came to agree in their thinking were willing to be baptized in the Eder River, and thus effected an organization in the year 1708. These Brethren, from diverse areas of the Rhine Valley, settled near the small town of Schwarzenau in the province of Wittgenstein. (Figure 2) As refugees in a land depopulated by war they were granted asylum even though religious dissenters. (50:15)

This sect received various names, but among themselves they called each other "Brethren", taken from Matthew 23:8. To this day members often address each other by the term "Brother" or "Sister". The membership in totality came to be known as the "Brotherhood". Because of their mode of baptism by immersion, outsiders called them "Baptists", a word of Greek origin. The German word "Dunker" has the same meaning. The word "Dunkard" is a perversion with connotations unacceptable to the Brethren. (12:186)

The Brethren were seeking relevance in religion for their day. They believed that the religious teachings of the time had strayed from the truth as found in the scriptures and as practiced by the first century church. Being one of the later groups of the Reformation, they studied not only the scriptures, but also the statements of other protesting groups. The early beliefs of the Brethren were eclectic in that they were drawn from the basic tenets of Christianity and of Protestantism, and sorted from the beliefs of the other groups. They were dialectic in that they attempted to resolve the tensions between these divergent modes of thought. (119:63)

14

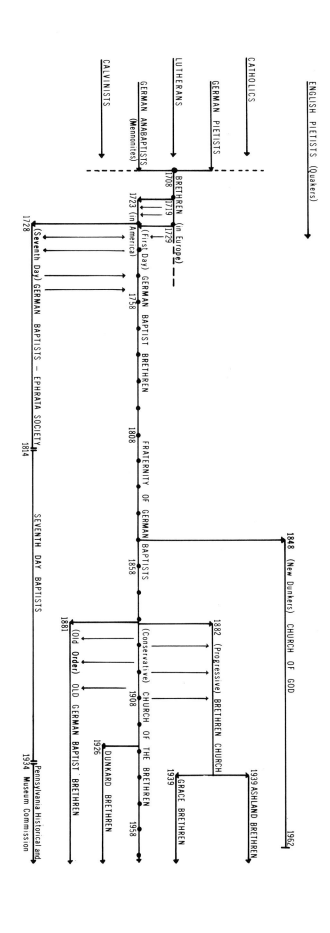

Figure 1. Time Line of Brethren History Showing Events and Divisions Within the Membership.

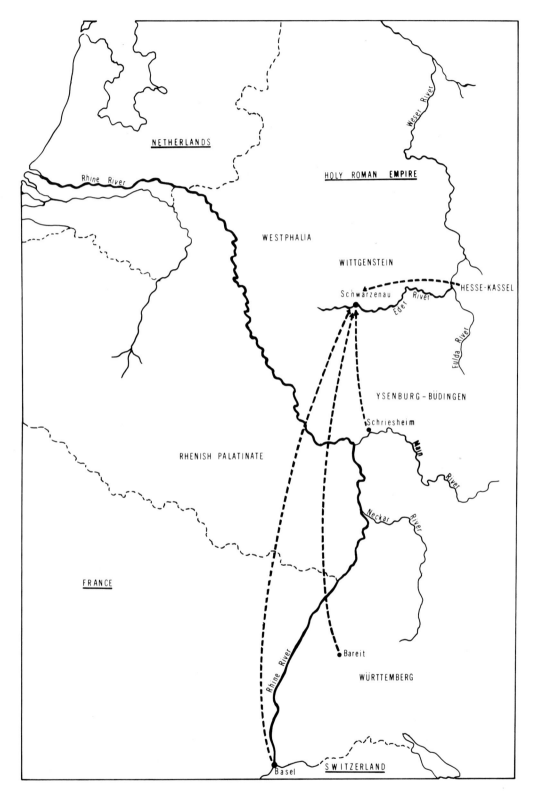

Figure 2. Locales of the Eight Charter Members Prior to Organization of the Church at Schwarzenau, Germany, 1708.

The Brethren were "Separatists" in that they separated themselves from the state churches: the Catholic, Lutheran, and Reformed. (13:35) This automatically meant the loss of all civil rights. They further separated themselves from civil government by refusing to bear arms and swear oaths, subjecting themselves only to their Heavenly King. However, they were obedient to the civil government wherein it did not infringe on their rights of conscience. (13:376) They separated themselves from the world in that they believed the purpose of mortal life was to make preparation for the eternal. This belief was to be expressed in a manner of living which differed from that of the nonbeliever.

The Brethren were "Anabaptists" in that they renounced their infant baptism and were rebaptized upon voluntary affirmation of faith. The Brethren accepted the warmth and zeal of "Mysticism". Their desire to establish a personal relationship with God necessitated freeing oneself from worldly cares to give time to spiritual matters. As a result of the Pietistic influence, the Brethren adopted no creed other than the New Testament and remained open to new truths from its teachings. Furthermore, they believed that divine revelation was possible at any time to any person. As new truth became evident, it could be incorporated in their ideology. (174:144)

The unique synthesis of these beliefs through human dialogue into a common faith, manifested the genius of these early Brethren. The beliefs distinctive to the Brethren were that there should be:

1. no force in religion;
2. a believer's baptism by trine immersion;
3. a literal obedience to the teachings of Christ;
4. an organized body of believers;
5. observance of the feet washing service, the Lord's Supper, and the Eucharist;
6. the kiss of charity;
7. the anointing of the sick;
8. the laying on of hands;
9. non-resistance and a refusal to bear arms;
10. a refusal to take oaths;
11. marriage only between believers, the bond of which was not to be broken;
12. divine revelation consistent with New Testament teachings; and
13. a final restoration of all men, with none being sent to eternal perdition. (174:138+)

The Brethren organized a body of believing Christians separate from the state. They considered the training of members in the way of the church as their primary function and the exercising of disciplinary power as secondary. They assumed the authority to both admit and dismiss members from the offices they had created. The polity of the Brethren was an outgrowth of two chapters of scripture, Matthew 18 and Acts 15. They attempted to keep the church pure through the use of avoidance and excommunication. The discipline that was administered was done with the purpose of restoring the individual to the fellowship.

After the founding of the first society at Schwarzenau in Wittgenstein, a second was formed at Marienborn in Ysenburg, and a third at Eppstein in the Lower Palatinate. Influence spread farther west to Krefeld in the Duchy of Cleves, under the rule of the King of Prussia; farther north into the Netherlands; and farther south into Switzerland. (34:38) As the number of new converts increased, alarm spread through the communities. The Brethren were persecuted on charges pressed by the state church and enforced by civil authorities. Persecution resulted in the migration of many members to America from 1719 to 1733. The Brethren followed many other immigrants who sought religious freedom, economic security, and a life of peace free from war conditions. (126:57+)

America, 1719-1800

Early Colonial Pennsylvania became a patchwork of religious and ethnic subcultural groups. Communities were settled by clusters of families who had migrated together. Each group attempted to preserve its own customs and ideals, and each resisted assimilation. (54:199)

Mennonites from Krefeld, Germany, established the first German settlement in America in 1682 at Germantown, Pennsylvania, six miles northwest of Philadelphia. The Brethren followed the route of the Mennonites and settled among them. In 1723 the Brethren organized a church at Germantown. Other Brethren had settled on the Schuylkill River and organized the Coventry and the Conestoga churches the next year. (4:179) From this third congregation members left the way of the Brethren to enter a life of mysticism, celibacy, and communal living at the Ephrata Cloister on Cocalico Creek.

Alexander Mack, Sr., the founder of the church in Germany, arrived in Germantown in 1729. With him came other Brethren who were forced to go from sixty to eighty miles west of Philadelphia to find unassigned land. This brought them into Lancaster County just east of the Susquehanna River. The main growth of the church stemmed from this area moving eastward into New Jersey and Maryland, southward along the ridges into the Shenandoah Valley of Virginia, and westward into Ohio, Kentucky, and Tennessee. (138:90) The Brethren continued their missionary activities, and by the Revolutionary War forty-six churches were established with a membership of fifteen hundred. (12:174) Brethren arrived before statehood for these respective territories and thus were true pioneers in helping to push back the Western frontier. (Figure 3)

The Brethren immigrants had some education. They could read the Bible in High German, but German was not the official language in America. A few private schools were located in Germantown. Mention should be made of two printers in Germantown–Christopher Sauer, Sr., not a member of the church, and Christopher Sauer, Jr., an elder of the Germantown church. From their press came three editions of the Bible, German newspapers, and other literature, which swayed the thinking of the German populace in regard to civic affairs. (12:386) Education was not opposed *per se*, but was meager on the frontier.

Local churches conducted their business meetings on a week day because Sunday was reserved for preaching. Even though all members were considered to be of equal status, the offices of service designated a hierarchy. Members were elected to office by a vote of the membership. Offices were those of the deaconry and ministry. There were three degrees of the ministry. Upon election a brother was allowed to preach. With advancement he was permitted to perform the rites of baptism and marriage. Upon ordination he became a "bishop" or "elder" and was granted all the rights and privileges of the office. Then he was eligible to be given the oversight of a local congregation and conduct the communion service. (16:49)

The Annual Meeting originated in 1742 in response to the activities of another religious group. The decision of the Brethren was not to participate in any phase of church union. They feared being caught in the snares of infant baptism and other doctrines which they had rejected at the founding of the church in Europe. (4:474) The Brethren decided, moreover, to hold such a meeting yearly, which has been called "Yearly Meeting", "Annual Meeting", and then "Annual Conference" after 1900. However, meetings were not held yearly, and minutes either were not kept or not preserved for all those held before 1830. These meetings consisted of two parts, exhortation and counseling. Queries were brought before the group, and cases were discussed in face to face confrontation. (34:165) All members had the right to vote. Later, necessity required the appointment of a

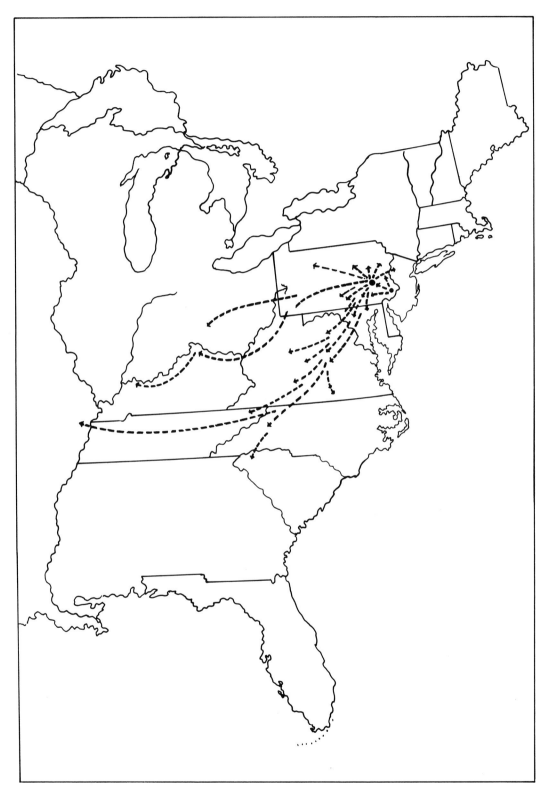

Figure 3. Migration of the Brethren in America During the Eighteenth Century.

committee to review the items of business being presented to the group as a whole. This committee was the forerunner of Standing Committee in the next century. (34:169) These meetings were held in a central location at first. As the membership increased, it became necessary to rotate the place of the meeting.

The number of German immigrants to America continued to increase until they outnumbered those from England. In 1727 the Pennsylvania Provincial Assembly became alarmed, lest the Germans would become a majority and take over the province. Therefore it required all German immigrants to take an Oath of Allegiance to King George II and to conform to the civil laws prescribed by both England and the Assembly. (44:9) Persecution took its toll once more among the Brethren during the Revolutionary War. The Brethren held beliefs in opposition to the beliefs of the populace and again found themselves in tension with society at large. They refused to break their oaths of loyalty, to participate in military violence, or to go to law. The Brethren were willing to affirm the Oath of Allegiance to the English crown as required of German immigrants. They were willing to be obedient to a civil government which had granted them religious and economic freedom. Consequently, they were reluctant to become naturalized citizens and to take part in any politics which was in opposition to England. (12:255) Thus some were accused of being Tories.

The eighteenth century ended with the membership scattered over many miles. The war had shattered their resources, destroyed the power of the Sauer press, and sent a peace-loving people out from the center of culture and government. The wilderness experience forced them to till the soil. Three-quarters of a century was required for them to regain their loss. (119:67) However, one historian wrote that the Brethren had gained their freedom. They were free to enjoy their possessions, their language, their civil rights, and their religion. They moved on into the next century of the church without a marked celebration.

America, 1801-1970

During the nineteenth century the growth of the church was by two processes, immigration and recruitment. The Brethren now perceived the "good life" as that lived on the land. In their search for new land they followed the routes taken by other settlers going West. Being opposed to slavery, they sought land in free states. (90:78) (Figure 4.) By 1836 the Brethren came to use the name "Fraternity of German Baptists" for official land titles. The farther west the Brethren went, the more of their German character they lost. (138:95)

By 1825 the English language began to replace German in the state of Pennsylvania, but it did not come into general use until 1840. (18:527) German lingered much longer among the Brethren. German and English were both used for preaching at least as late as 1879. (117:29) A few elderly members in long established churches were observed exchanging greetings in German as late as 1970.

The Brethren came to believe that they had the "truth". Their faith had been tested and proven, and they wanted to preserve it as the "right" way of living. Having retained a set of beliefs which were in opposition to the world, they limited their interaction with society at large and thus reduced the tension between themselves and society. Increased interaction within the group developed a community of spirit. They felt that the continuance of their way of life, including the church, depended upon the perpetuation of the group. Factors which promoted isolation and separation from the world were: the adoption of agriculture as a vocation; settlement in closely knit groups; the development of an identity as a social and religious group; and a literal interpretation of the Bible, fostering beliefs manifested in separation from the world.

20

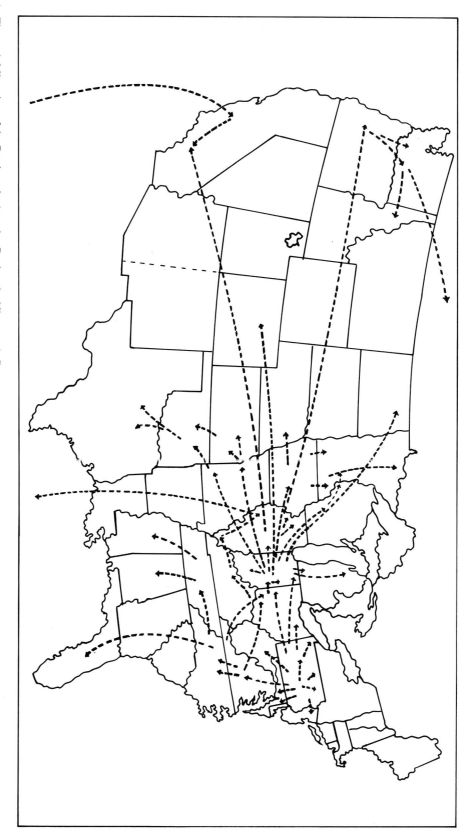

Figure 4. Migration of the Brethren in America During the Nineteenth Century.

The problem of the Brethren was to keep the church pure, or "Brethren", and not to lose the ground that they had gained by separation. An oft-quoted scripture was Romans 12:2, "...be not conformed to this world, but be ye transformed..." Conformity was to be in terms of the Brethren way of life rather than of the world. In all sincerity the Brethren set up rules to perfect their way of life and thus developed a "casuistry" within the church. This term is defined as: "the solving of special cases of right and wrong in conduct by applying general principles of ethics, and deciding how far circumstances alter cases". (55)

The polity of the church was expanded and refined during the nineteenth century. The governing bodies at the local, district, and national levels were called on to make decisions on new issues and to defend prior decisions. The polity of a local church was congregational in affairs which concerned it alone. It had the authority to admit and dismiss members, and to elect and remove a member from office. Each member in "full fellowship" was entitled to one vote at church council meeting. Women were allowed to vote as well as men, even though they did not exercise the right to the same extent. (34:280)

The offices for service were the deaconry and ministry, held for life. Offices were filled without nomination. The member receiving a plurality during voting was installed. Women were licensed to preach, but were not advanced further in office. (34:280) The three degrees of the ministry were much the same as those listed for the eighteenth century. (4:391)

An elder was given the oversight of a local congregation when elected to do so by members in council. The elder who had the greatest seniority usually held this position until death. (34:282) As items of business became apparent, the presiding elder or "housekeeper" called a council meeting, which convened on a week day. Any lay member could raise a question from the floor for group discussion and vote if needed.

If the matter merited the attention of the Brotherhood, it was formulated into a query. This query was then placed in the hands of a delegate or elder who presented it to the next higher authoritative body. (90:111)

Attendance at early Annual Meetings was voluntary on the part of lay members, but all ministers and elders were expected to attend. Any member in attendance had a right to vote. By 1847 representation consisted of two delegates from each congregation, received by written credentials. The delegate body received and examined all queries. A two-thirds vote was required for the adoption of a query. (90:117) The minutes of the Annual Meeting are available for every year from 1830 to date. The *Full Report* is available from 1876 to 1930. Stenographers were hired to record every word of the business sessions, including those of each speaker on the floor. These minutes have proved to be a valuable resource in documenting this investigation.

A query came to the Annual Meeting of 1856 requesting the privilege of forming territorial districts in order to lessen the business to be carried on at Annual meeting and to provide a means of settling difficulties at an intermediate level. (90:196) Queries which originated within a local congregation were then sent to the district meeting. Local churches appointed delegates to district meeting as well as to Annual Meeting. Standing Committee was composed of delegates elected by each district during their respective meetings.

The use of discipline in the church had two aspects–the pointing out of error that the church might be kept pure (59:233+) and the settling of differences between individuals, between an individual and a group, or between groups. Error consisted of departing from that which was required by the New Testament and came to include that which departed from the Brethren way of life.

Admonishment was the duty of both the elder

in charge of the congregation and all members of the group. It was done generally by sermons given to the congregation as a whole and personally by approaching an individual in private. Differences between two individuals were to be settled privately, according to Matthew 18. They were to be brought before the church in council only if a settlement could not be reached, or if the issue involved a point of doctrine or the authority of the church. (59:233+)

After admonishing a person and observing no change in his behavior, the presiding elder or another person was to bring the case before the church council. The offender was to be notified, to be present, and to make any testimony he desired. The determination of the offense, its seriousness, and verdict was the duty of the local church. Avoidance and excommunication were to be used as a last resort, only if the digressor were unwilling to change his ways after having been admonished. (59:233+)

Partial avoidance consisted of excluding the offender from the kiss of charity, the right to vote in church council, and the communion service. Complete avoidance or excommunication consisted of being excluded from all interaction with other persons in the group. Since the action of the church council was required to place a person in avoidance, its action was required to reinstate him. Upon reinstatement all privileges of membership were restored, but not those of office unless so stated. A transference of membership required a "letter" or certificate from his home congregation stating that he was a member in "good standing". (59:233+)

If the party involved had grievances, he could ask for a rehearing of the case. Then the presiding elder could call for assistance from elders in adjoining congregations. For the adjustment of difficulties which could not be settled within a local church, an individual or a church group had recourse to the district

meeting. A committee would be appointed by the officers of the district to investigate the case and make its report. If rejected, it was possible for a local congregation to appeal to Annual Meeting for assistance in the settling of difficulties. When requested, the Standing Committee selected three or five disinterested elders to appear at the local council meeting and review the case. The resulting decision was final. An issue developing out of a case of discipline could be restated as a query to be passed on to Annual Meeting for a decision applicable to like cases in the future. (59:233+)

In 1850 the authority of Annual Meeting was brought into question. The decision of the voting body was that its decisions should be obeyed until changed by that body. (90:144) In 1860 the question of authority was answered in that the decisions of Annual Meeting were to be made a "test of fellowship". This meant that, if a person did not conform, he was subject to excommunication. The rules of Annual Meeting had been placed equal in authority with the scriptures. (90:241) This action resulted in further difficulties and test cases which extended over many years.

Division within the membership of the church body was not new in the nineteenth century, but it was new to each generation of churchmen that dealt with it. The greatest schism came in the 1880's in regard to "progressive" and "old order" factions within the church. Gillin wrote that social conditions had created two radically different views within the church. (19:24) The Old Order Brethren viewed the situation as one in which the church had departed too far from the old ways. Important matters were not being made a test of fellowship. Changes had brought about a "corruption of the ordinances". Changes were being made in the time honored decisions of Annual Meeting. (36:26) Reconciliation did not come out of the dialogues of the Annual meeting of 1881. Instead the Old Order Brethren organized as a separate body and called themselves the "Old German Baptist Brethren". (see Figure 1.)

From the Progressive Brethren viewpoint the church was not keeping up with the times. The traditions and customs which had developed within the life of the church could not be defended by the Gospel and therefore were not considered to be valid. Many rules passed by Annual Meeting were considered to be based on tradition rather than scripture. The issue became heated when these rules were made a test of fellowship. These members felt that force was being used in religion, and the right of conscience was being ignored. Progressive Brethren called a meeting in 1882 and effected an organization in 1883. They adopted as their name the "Brethren Church". (36:26) They rejected the mode of dress which was continued by the other two groups. In the eyes of the Conservative Brethren, who took a position between these two extremes, the Old Order Brethren were holding back the growth of the church, and the Progressive Brethren were moving too fast on unsure ground. (see Figure 1) The Conservative Brethren retained the name "German Baptist Brethren", which had formerly been used by all. In 1908 they officially changed their name to "Church of the Brethren". (91:872) (see Figure 1) Since this investigation has been limited to the Church of the Brethren, information concerning the other two groups has been eliminated at this point in time.

The publications of the Brethren were few in the early part of the nineteenth century because of the destruction of the Sauer press. In 1850 the interest in publishing was renewed and gradually increased. Publications consisted of Bibles, hymnbooks, minutes of the Annual Meetings, periodicals, almanacs, tracts, and Sunday school lesson helps, almost all in English. Particularly helpful in documenting this research were the minutes of the Annual Meetings and three periodicals–*The Gospel Visitor, Christian Family Companion,* and *The*

Gospel Messenger.

At one time education beyond common school was frowned upon by some Brethren. As the Brethren moved into vocations other than farming, some members changed their views with regard to education. A need was felt to establish parochial schools to provide secular and religious training at the college level within a religious environment. Of the thirty-two academies, normal schools, colleges, seminaries, and industrial institutes attempted by the Brethren, seven accredited institutions have remained–six liberal arts colleges and a seminary. (35:178) Regardless of their degree of success these institutions of higher learning provided new leadership for the church and made an impact on the public schools and other professions.

Home mission work was not new to the Brethren in this century, but foreign mission work was. Mission work was opened in Denmark in 1875, in Asia Minor and India in 1895. Other attempts were made in Switzerland and France. Missionary activities in the church reached an all time high by the time of the bicentennial celebration in 1908. (43:282) Missions have been established in China, Nigeria, Puerto Rico, and Ecuador.

The changes in the pattern of the American culture were reflected in the life of the church. Gradually the Brethren lost characteristics which designated them as a sect and took on those of a church. The membership has rejected in part its past isolation from society and the legalism which had developed as an attempt to perpetuate this way of life. Yet members find it difficult to fully align themselves with the trends in the present society. New methods of transportation and communication permit interaction with people far beyond the boundaries of the former small rural communities. (32:38) The "good life" is no longer conceived of as only that lived on the farm. Many members enter vocations other than farming. They follow the shifts in population toward the city and out to the suburbs. They obtain more formal and informal education. They belong to the middle socio-economic class. New trends of thought have made for differences between groups within the church. In spite of the diversity, many seek a "unity of spirit" among a membership of over 200,000 across the nation and at mission and service projects around the world. (137:140) (Figure 5)

In an age of change the church can no longer provide a definite answer for every daily problem. Members are given the privilege of making their own decisions in response to their own conscience under the guidance of their own congregation. (45:24) The practice of admonishing an individual has become a personal matter. Avoidance and excommunication are no longer practiced openly, but removal from office has continued. Offenders are not excluded from the fellowship, but are to be shown love and forbearance. The reason for this change is that the fellowship and counsel of the church are to be available; the power of redemption is to be expressed through love. The duty of the church is perceived as not judging sinners, but proclaiming the love of God and His forgiveness of sin to all mankind.

The voting body of the church at Annual Meeting has become a delegate assembly prorated by the number of members per congregation. Membership on Standing Committee and the officers of conference as well as those of the local church have been opened to the laity, both men and women. Queries reflect a wider concern about societal problems. Standing Committee has chosen not to provide answers to queries as it formerly did, but to await response on the part of the delegate body and the membership at large. Many of the rules which were made a test of fellowship are no longer observed,

although not all have been struck from the minutes of Annual Meeting.

The Brethren have adopted a new view of society, a society which they can serve and with which they can share the hope that lies within them. In seeking its new identity the church continues to seek a synthesis of the movements which were its genius at the time of its founding. With an enlarged view of the world the beliefs of the members have enlarged. The beliefs of the Brethren today are perceived as follows:

1. that the New Testament is their rule of faith and practice, although a more liberal interpretation has been adopted;
2. that God continues to reveal himself to man, and man is able to establish a relationship with him;
3. that an organized church is able both to nurture and to provide opportunities for service;
4. that the message of the church is God's redeeming love and the forgiveness of sin, bringing hope and reconciliation to all mankind;
5. that through a personal discipline, spiritual values transcend all others;
6. that there is to be no force in religion, and a decision of conscience by another person is to be respected; and
7. that life is to be lived in terms of today's world rather than that of the first, the eighteenth, or the nineteenth centuries. (3:131)

Emphasis is placed on keeping the church "Christian", and then keeping it "Brethren". The Brethren are attempting: to extract the "good" from their heritage, to follow the truths in the New Testament, to find a purpose for daily living, and to have a concern for neighbor.

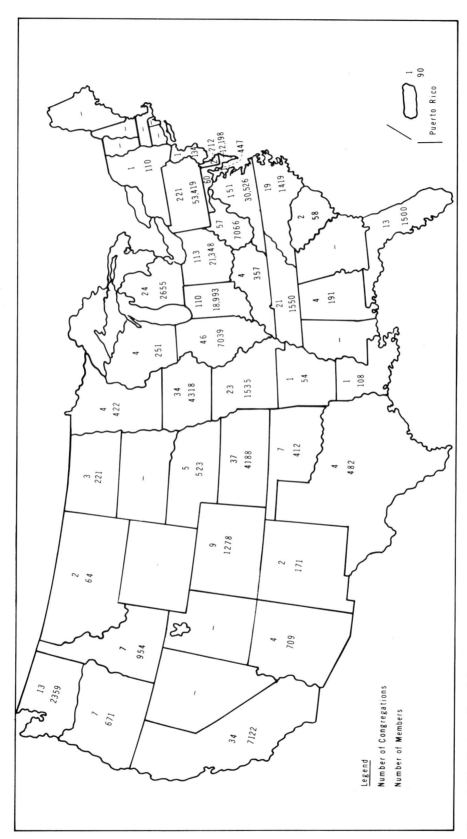

Figure 5. Distribution of Local Congregations and Membership by States, 1970.

Chapter 4

HISTORY OF THE DRESS WORN BY THE MEMBERS OF THE CHURCH OF THE BRETHREN

The cultural setting and religious beliefs held by the members of the Church of the Brethren throughout their history have been significant factors in determining their mode of dress. The Brethren in Europe wore the dress of the peasant and artisan class of the locales of their diverse origins. In America, as a subcultural group, they synthesized a mode of dress which expressed their life style and signified membership in this socio-religious group. Specific items of clothing were prescribed for the brethren and the sisters. Changes made in these items were evident with the passage of time. Hierarchies of adoption and demise were noted. Although the majority of the members no longer adhere to the prescribed dress, a few members had retained it as late as 1970.

Dress in Europe, 1708-1733

Clothing is not thought to have been a major issue in the deliberations at the origin of the church. A notation concerning the riches of the world was made by the founder, Alexander Mack, Sr., in his Bible. Translated it reads, "Has it not been ordained that men have the best things in common such as life and body? Thus the wealthiest people in this world have a small advantage only in the lowliest things, such as food and clothing." (12:420) Mack's other writings were concerned with doctrines and ordinances. (101) A Brethren historian reported an incident concerning Mack. An inquiring neighbor questioned Mack concerning the garb to be worn by the members of his new group. Mack answered, "They shall be recognized by the manner of their living." (2:91)

The assumption has been made by the author that the Brethren did not prescribe a uniform mode of dress during the period in Europe for at least four reasons. Since the Brethren believed that there should be no force in religion, a prescribed mode of dress as a requirement for membership in the group would have been considered a violation of this belief. Secondly, a distinctive dress would have identified them as dissenters, resulting in even greater persecution from civil and state church authorities. Thirdly, the eight charter members were drawn from three different localities in the Rhine Valley and from Switzerland. Since the membership reached one thousand over this twenty-five year period, it hardly seems possible that a mode of costume could have been synthesized under these conditions. Lastly, the acquisition of specific items of dress required the laying aside of those on hand. As refugees, they would not have had the means to secure the required items of clothing. (4:546)

The Brethren were drawn from the artisan and peasant classes and wore the socio-economic class dress of their locale. Although specific evidence has not been found regarding the items of clothing worn by the Brethren in Europe, an assumption concerning their clothing has been made by the author from her study of European costume in general. A brother wore a beard and long hair, perhaps reaching to the shoulder. He wore a linen shirt, knee breeches, long stockings, heavy shoes, and a broad-brimmed black felt hat. A less well-to-do member wore a long-sleeved jacket which reached slightly below the waist and a plain shirt. If means permitted, a brother may have worn an unadorned long coat, called a justacorps, with perhaps a ruffled shirt for dress occasions.

A sister fashioned her long hair into a bun. Her clothing consisted of a one- or two-piece dress with fitted bodice, fitted long sleeves, and gathered skirt; a neckerchief or fichu, or both; an apron; a cap; shoes and stockings; and perhaps a hooded cloak for inclement weather. An artist's conception of the dress of the eight charter members and other early Brethren is shown in Figures 6A, 6B, and 6C.

Dress in America, 1719-1800

The plain dress of the German Pietists in Pennsylvania originated in a different period of time from that of the English Pietists, or Quakers, who settled Philadelphia. In writing about Colonial costume the authors Warwick, Pitz, and Wyckoff made a general statement about the dress developed by the various groups of German origin.

> In a general way, the same principles... can be applied to that of the various sects of German Pietists. They too were "plain people", frowning upon anything that smacked of ostentation. Yet although they all worked toward an ideal of simplicity, each sect had its own restrictions and prohibitions and differed from the others in minor ways... all worked out the problems of plain dressing in their own way... Once these groups found a type of dress expressing their ideal of plainness, they held to it tenaciously, allowing few changes to be made. This was all the more possible, since living in a district of their own, they were isolated from the rest of the colony. Some of these groups have maintained their

integrity to this day. (54:201)

Discussion of Brethren dress in Colonial America has been divided in three parts: the dress of the Brethren as German immigrants, the dress worn by adherents of the Ephrata Society, and the dress of the Brethren who lived on the frontier. Records are meager and the information is very general. Illustrations for this period are shown in Figures 7 through 17.

Dress of Brethren Immigrants

Many of the immigrants who settled at Germantown outside Philadelphia had been expert weavers in Germany. The town became the center of the linen industry, which was further stimulated by the coming of the Scotch-Irish in 1728. (18:161) With the skills that the Brethren, who came in 1719 under the leadership of Peter Becker, had in textile production, surely they made a contribution. (16:71) Out of necessity they made their own clothing.

The author has not located to date any written or pictorial illustrations left by the Brethren living in this period, which describe with any specificity the dress they wore as immigrants. Furthermore no documents were located by this investigator at the Germantown Historical Society Library concerning the dress of German immigrants who settled in Germantown. Therefore it has been necessary to rely on the writing of Pennsylvania historians in general for information concerning dress and other incidents concerning the Brethren in particular.

The German immigrant was a farmer or day laborer, and his wife a domestic. A description of their clothing was given by Keyser.

> The farmer and laborer wore coarse linen shirts, flannel blouses, breeches of tanned deerskin, woolen stockings and neatskin shoes closely set with flat-headed nails driven into their heavy soles. In summer, children and many of their elders went barefoot. The artisan could be distinguished by his heavy leather apron

28

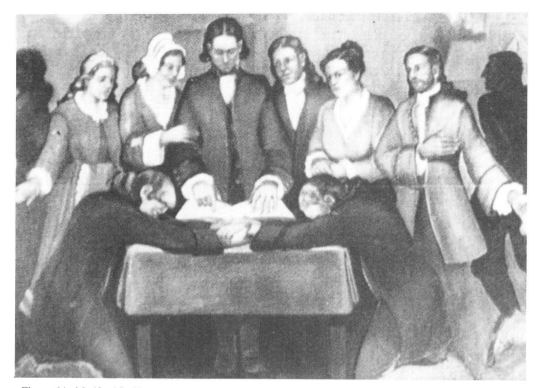

Figure 6A. Medford D. Neher. A Mural History of the Church of the Brethren. Camp Alexander Mack, Milford, Indiana. Panel I. Eight Charter Members.

Figure 6B. Panel I. Brethren Emigrants from Europe, 1719.

Figure 6C. Panel II. Brethren Immigrants to America, 1729.

reaching from his chest to below his knees. Caps and hats made from the skins of muskrat, raccoon or beaver, or three cornered hats of coarse wool, formed the favorite headgear of men and boys. The short dress of the woman was made of worsted, linsey-woolsey, or linen according to the season. On her head she wore a white cap, it being... a rare thing to see a bareheaded woman. (31:123)

Sunday afforded a time for dressing in more fashionable items of clothing, as means permitted its acquisition.

In writing on the early history of Pennsylvania, Fletcher made reference to the four social classes transplanted from Europe. Gentlemen were wealthy merchants and officeholders. Professional men were ministers and lawyers. Farmers, shopkeepers, and mechanics ranked third. Free laborers, indentured servants, and Negro slaves were last. (18:538) In writing about English costume in America, Earle stated, "Dress was also to the colonist an important badge of rank; and for many years class distinctions are carefully guarded and insisted upon in America as in England." (14:3) For a time, the immigrants were satisfied with their status in America because they had held the same in Europe.

Only fragments of information have been found about the dress of the Brethren who lived in Germantown. The Brethren historian, M.G. Brumbaugh, wrote, "There is no record to indicate that any distinctive dress was worn by the first comers to America." (4:547) The only description found concerning the dress of Alexander Mack, Jr., as a bishop of the Germantown Congregation, was given by an eyewitness.

> I became a member young, and well do I remember brother Alexander Mack perfectly well. When I was a little girl he visited my father... well do I remember his exceeding plainness of dress. He wore a broad brimmed hat and dressed very plain. (122:230)

Brumbaugh states further that the Brethren were influenced by Quaker dress.

> But here in Pennsylvania the Quaker hat and bonnet became the symbol of non-resisting people. Those who sided with the proprietary and against the council naturally adopted the dress of the Quakers, whence arose the head dress of the members. This gradual adoption of a distinctive garb was, of course, sanctioned by the membership generally as being in harmony with the principles of the Gospel. (4:547)

The conclusion has been drawn by the author that the dress of the Brethren as immigrants was the same as the dress of other German immigrants. Thus a brother wore a beard and a long hair style, possibly reaching the shoulders. He wore a long-sleeved jacket, reaching slightly below the waist, a linen shirt, and knee breeches. Accessories included long white stockings, heavy shoes, and a broad-brimmed hat, with perhaps a round crown. If means permitted, he wore a frilled shirt and a long coat, called a justacorps, with or without a standing collar. A sister fashioned her long hair into a bun. Her outer clothing consisted of a one- or two-piece dress with fitted bodice, long fitted sleeves, and long gathered skirt, worn without hoops. The dress fabrics were plain in modest colors. Her accessories included a neckerchief, a fichu, an apron, and a white cap. During inclement weather perhaps she added a cloak with attached hood. If worn at all, the bonnet was not adopted until very late in the eighteenth century.

A mural painting of the printshop of Christopher Sauer, Sr., in 1745 is shown in Figure 7. Since no sketches of the printshop are known to exist, the artist chose to dress Sauer and his associates in a manner typical of early printers in America. (202) The portraits of Peter Keyser and wife, members of the Germantown church, show them attired in Colonial dress, although the portraits may have been painted in the next

30

Figure 7. Barnard C. Taylor. Christopher Sauer's Printing Shop, Germantown. Beeghley Library, Juniata College, Huntingdon, Pennsylvania.

century. (Figures 8 and 9). The caps shown in Figures 10 and 11 belonged to this sister. The plainer one, made of a sheer woven linen, has a wide frontlet, or brim, and relatively small crown. The ties are an extension of the frontlet. A pleasing decorative touch was added by the application of a heavy thread about one inch from the front edge. The slightly more decorative cap, made of bobbinette, has a ruffle along the edge of the frontlet and across the back of the neck.

A portrait of Joseph Mueller (1707-1761) is shown in Figure 12. Durnbaugh is of the opinion that Mueller retained Brethren dress although he left the group.

> Although Müller joined the Moravians, evidently he persisted in Brethren dress despite his membership in the other group. I say this, because the curator of the Moravian archives at Herrnhut in Eastern Germany indicated that Müller's portrait was different from all the other paintings of Moravians in their collection. (181)

The portrait shows Mueller wearing long hair, a beard, and mustache. The coat appears to be in the fashion of the late eighteenth century with its standing collar and decorative buttons and buttonholes.

Dress of the Ephrata Society

The mode of dress associated with membership of the Ephrata Cloister probably was not adopted immediately. The pilgrims, perhaps on a journey to visit the Brethren at Germantown, did not wear the habit worn at the Cloister in later years. (Figure 13) They wore broad-brimmed round-crowned hats. Although it is not possible to distinguish much detail in this illustration, much similarity in dress is noted. The same style of hat was observed in the artist's sketch of an incident concerning the appearance of Michael Wohlfahrt at a public market in Philadelphia to denounce the citizenry. (Figure 14) He was a hermit on Cocalico Creek and

in sympathy with the teachings at the Cloister.

In time the dress worn at the Ephrata Cloister differed greatly from that worn by the Brethren. A habit was adopted by both the single sisters and brothers at the Cloister and also by the householders who lived in the surrounding community. It was similar to that worn by Capuchin monks. (99:5) Figure 15 shows this habit reproduced from one of the old manuscripts printed at the Cloister. The habit was donned at baptism. A person's intentions to leave the order were visibly announced to the others by his removal of the habit. (5:228) The conclusion has been drawn by this investigator that the habit worn at the Cloister did not influence the mode of dress worn by the Brethren. In fact the adoption of a habit made for even greater distinction in dress between the inhabitants of the Cloister and the Brethren living at Germantown and in the surrounding community.

Dress of the Brethren on the Frontier

The Brethren on the frontier adapted the dress of the German immigrant to their new environment. The wearing of homespun and heavy leather shoes gave evidence of living a life away from the luxuries of imports and the influence of the changes in fashionable dress. On weekdays a brother wore a plain shirt, a short jacket, and knee breeches of homespun or buckskin. If means permitted, he wore a cutback long coat with a simple white shirt and either breeches or trousers on Sunday. Brethren believed in nonviolence and therefore wore the symbolic clothing of other peace-loving sects in Pennsylvania. The long hair, the broad-brimmed hat, and the beard designated men holding pacifistic beliefs. The Brethren rejected the wearing of a mustache alone because it was a practice of the militia.

Not only was the dress of the Brethren adapted to meet their surroundings, but also their meeting houses. Since the men's hats were removed during worship services, the plain architecture of

32

Figure 8. Colonial Dress, Peter Keyser, Bishop of
Germantown Church.

Figure 9. Colonial Dress, Catherine Clemens Keyser.

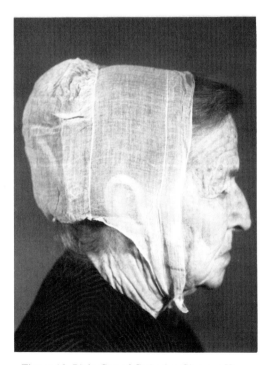

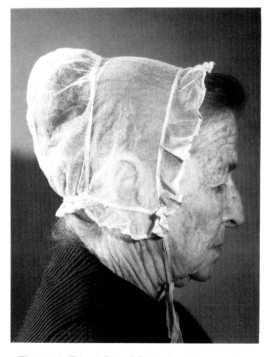

Figure 10. Plain Cap of Catherine Clemens Keyser.

Figure 11. Edged Cap of Catherine Clemens Keyser.

Figure 12. Hair and Coat Styles of Joseph Mueller (1707-1761).

Figure 13. Early Dress of Brothers at Ephrata Cloister.

34

Figure 14. Round-Crowned Hat, Michael Wohlfahrt.

Figure 15. A Sister's Garb at Ephrata Cloister.

Figure 16. Hat Board, Price Town Meeting House.

the meeting house provided a means of storage. A board was dropped from the ceiling, parallel to the center aisle. Wooden pegs were inserted on each side to hold the broad-brimmed hats. (Figure 16)

The sisters on the frontier wore the dress described for the sister living at Germantown. The retention of plain dress was promoted for two reasons according to Brumbaugh. The fashionable hoop skirts adopted by society women in Philadelphia were denounced by Christopher Sauer in his newspaper. (4:547) During the Revolutionary War the Colonists voluntarily gave up the wearing of patterned fabrics from England. The wearing of homespun fabric of one color became patriotic. After the war, "especially those active in the war, reverted to stylish dress. In this the plain people of God found added reason for retaining simplicity. Why should they follow the example in dress of the people whose example in war they did not follow?" (4:548) The sisters in the church did not wear hoops or patterned fabrics. Therefore a distinction arose between their dress and that of the world.

The only illustration located of the Brethren who lived on the frontier during this century was a pen sketch made a century later. The artist's sketch shows members entering the Coventry Church in Chester County, Pennsylvania, before 1800. (Figure 17) Since the increase in membership of the church stemmed from this church and other rural churches, rather than from the Germantown Church, frontier dress became the dominant mode of the Brethren by the end of the eighteenth century.

Prescribed Dress, 1801-1970

An interesting phenomenon occurred early in the nineteenth century. The length of time a mode of dress was in fashion became shorter than the average life span of a man. As a subcultural group in an isolated setting, the Brethren were slow to make changes in their dress, retaining much of the basic style worn during the previous century. With the more frequent changes in fashionable dress the difference between it and Brethren dress became progressively more noticeable. During this time a particular mode of dress developed and signified membership in this particular religious sect.

By 1900 the walls of isolation were crumbling, increasing the vulnerability of the way of life of the Brethren to outside influences transmitted by new communication and transportation media. An evangelistic spirit among the membership and an educated clergy and laity, located in both rural and urban settings, resulted in changes in the life of the church and in views held by the membership. Changes were reflected in the prescribed dress and its significance. Both the brethren and the sisters gradually laid aside items of clothing which signified church membership and adopted items of fashionable dress.

Attitudes Favoring Plainness in Dress

At the beginning of the nineteenth century the Brethren were a free people. They owned land in their own right. They could worship in their own way. They were granted civil protection. They sought to maintain the freedom they had gained. Graeff wrote that a society tends to retain the way of life followed at the time it gained its freedom. (20:82) Rather than adapting to social changes about them the Brethren clung to a mode of life which soon became the past. In time they found that this way of life was in opposition to that of the world.

The Brethren strove to express their beliefs in every aspect of daily living. Their "plain dress" became a visual statement of their beliefs. As they sought unity within the group, the wide variations in this plainness became an issue. "Nonconformity to the world" came to mean "conformity to the mode of dress" worn by the group.

"Pride" was denounced by the Bible. During

Figure 17. Dress of Members of Coventry Church, Pennsylvania, c. 1800.

this time the word "fashion" came to be synonymous with the word "pride". (189) This use of the term implied an attitude and conduct which reflected superiority or contempt, an unwillingness to perform tasks below one's station in life, and an expression of sexual desires, especially female. (41:1350) Thus the adoption of the fashions of the world came to mean sinful living, which was inconsistent with the Christian way of life. Pride was to be overcome by prayer and self-denial. It was inferred that a person who did not dress "plain" did not practice these virtues.

Members of families who had not become members of the church attended services dressed in the fashion of the day. Their appearance reminded those in plain dress of the difference between the member and the non-member. The person in fashionable dress could hardly go unnoticed by others. The turning of a church service into a fashion show was renounced by a sister in Virginia. She wrote that the scripture commanded the assembling of believers together, but for purposes other than "show". Such persons would be held accountable on the Judgment Day. (57:9)

The mode of dress which developed among the Brethren came to be known as the "order of dress". This terminology was shortened to fewer words– "in the order" or "in order". Even though there were changes in the order of dress the term meant the prescribed dress worn at a particular time.

The appearance of the Brethren dressed in the order has been described by secular writers, especially during the news coverage of the Annual Meetings. A description of the brethren was found for the Annual Meeting of 1852 held south of Goshen, Indiana.

> I must acknowledge that the sight of so many apparently devout and unassuming members, led on by the example of the gray headed fathers among them all so plainly

dressed, with their long beards helping to mark the whole external man with an air of dignity and devotion. (142:17)

A description of the sisters was found in *Scribner's Magazine* for November, 1901.

> They have fine faces, the women of these simple sects, and the austere scoop bonnet and the kerchief at the neck almost seem a fitting frame for the placid countenance of the bishop's helpmate. Her dress, too, is plain in color and cut and is unornamented by frills or furbelows. (136:514)

Other writers, more familiar with the group, were quick to mention differences and inconsistencies found in the dress of the Brethren. An observer of the Philadelphia Congregation wrote in 1869.

> I have been to the Meeting here several times... They have a very plain Meeting house, they themselves are not so plain as might be desired. (179)

One elder was loved and respected in spite of his shortcomings. A description reads:

> He was always in demand as a preacher; there was always a place for him... His cane and his pipe were his ever-present companions. Unlike most elders in the Brethren Church, he played the fiddle. He was a man of medium height, had straight, black hair, and always wore a pleasant smile. He was not particular in the form of his dress, yet intended to conform to the order of the Brotherhood. (6:199)

Tobacco and musical instruments were frowned upon by the Brethren. The prescribed dress and neat appearance which personified other brethren were lacking. The outsider recognized the difference between fashionable dress and plain dress. Furthermore the Brethren knew who were members in each local church and the stand each took in regard to the order of dress of the church.

Hair and Clothing Styles Worn by the Brethren

Evidence regarding the dress of this period indicated specific items of clothing which were worn and were required for church membership and for election to office. These items differed significantly from fashionable dress. A brother could be identified as a member of the church because of his dress. The dress of the brethren, shown in Figures 18 through 67, depict that worn after 1850 because photography was not available generally before this time and because it was prohibited by the church as late as 1904. However, some photographs were taken despite church rulings.

Hair and Beard. The manner of wearing the hair and beard was the most contested topic of the dress of men affiliated with the church during the nineteenth century and early part of the twentieth century. The first decision made at Annual Meeting regarding personal appearance was in 1804 concerning the beard. Article 5 asked whether a brother who had shaved off his beard might be ordained as a bishop. The answer was negative, accompanied by a three-fold reason. God made man with a beard. In Leviticus 21:5 man was commanded not to shave off his beard. Christ and the disciples provided an example by wearing a beard. (90:34)

Again in 1822, the question was asked whether a brother without a beard should be advanced to the second degree of the ministry. The answer was that a brother who could not deny himself in this matter should not be advanced. (90:59) The ruling must not have been adhered to in every respect for the issue was brought again before the Annual Meeting of 1846, and the former decision was retained. In addition Article 11 stated that conscientious members could not vote to advance a person in office who did not conform to the rule. (90:115) No accurate account has been located as to how many of the brethren did or did not wear a beard, but apparently there was considerable variance among them.

A glimpse of the hair style and beard worn by the brethren in the first half of the nineteenth century is shown in Figure 18, taken from Nead's *Theological Writings*, published in 1850. Apparently the hair of the brethren was not worn quite as long after 1850 as it had been earlier. Yet their hair style was readily distinguishable from fashionable styles. A verbal description of the manner of wearing the hair appeared in *Scribner's Magazine* in 1901.

> The bishop's hair is long, and is trimmed off straight, just below the ears, which causes it to stick out in a most inartistic fashion. His beard is long, too, and his upper lip is clean shaven, for among his people a moustache is a badge of worldliness. (136:513)

Article 8 of the minutes of 1864 stated that members were to be admonished by the ministering brethren if they did not conform to the order of the church in the wearing of the hair. If a member failed to comply after being admonished several times, he was to be dealt with according to Matthew 18. (90:280) A specified manner for dressing the hair was adopted in the minutes of 1866, Article 47.

> By plainness of dress, we mean the common order of giving shape to dress, as practiced by the old brethren and sisters generally, and by plainness of hair we mean the hair parted on top of the head, or all combed back in a plain manner, or combed straight down all around the head, and not having the hair and beard trimmed according to the custom of the world. (90:317)

Hair and beards worn to these specifications are shown in Figures 19 through 21. Reconsideration of the decision of 1866 was requested in 1868. Scriptural authority was sought for the position taken in regard to the beard. The answer revealed the attitude of those who phrased it, "Considered, that in absence of direct Scripture, it is well for the younger to be subject to the older".

Figure 18. Long Hair Style of the Brethren, c. 1850.

Figure 19. Hair Style, John L. Ullery (1814-1884).

Figure 20. Hair Style of a Brother Long.

Figure 21. Shorter Hair Style, Abraham Miller
(1809-1884).

(90:335) Surely the young brother shown in Figure 22 was complying with the regulation.

A query concerning the wearing of only a mustache was brought before the Annual Meeting of 1862. The decision reached in Article 11 was in two parts. A brother who trimmed neither his beard nor the hair on his upper lip for conscience sake was to be respected. If he chose to wear only the beard and shave his upper lip, that was his privilege. (90:257) (see Figures 19 through 21) The greatest objection came from wearing a mustache alone because it was the custom of the world and the militia. (12:221) Despite these regulations, some brethren apparently adopted the fashion of the world with liberty of conscience, declaring that the wearing of the mustache alone was "good for the eyes". Article 7, 1874, recorded that those who wore the mustache alone were subject to the "council of the church".

The mustache of some brethren was disagreeable when saluting another brother with the kiss of charity. If the kiss was ignored, this also caused a grievance. The answer given in Article 14 for 1869 stated that brethren should bear with one another, and continue to salute whether a mustache was or was not worn with the beard. (90:346) A further statement concerning the mustache was adopted by the Annual Meeting of 1888, Article 2. Brethren who did not clip their mustache and whose beard and mustache were unkempt were to be considered as "offenders and be dealt with accordingly". This meant that the kiss of charity would not be exchanged. A brother who was ignored was to take the hint that his mustache and beard were in need of care. (91:478)

Conformity to a particular manner of wearing the hair and beard was less of an issue when the styles prescribed for membership paralleled those worn by men of the world. Some brethren shingled their hair but retained the full beard with or without a mustache. (see Figures 23 through 25) Other brethren desired to remove

the beard as noted in an article which appeared in *The Gospel Messenger* in 1887.

> Years ago, but few brethren would wear a beard. Finally it became more fashionable, and the cross became less heavy. Now the beard is taken off, and the mustache is worn. The cross is getting too heavy for some of the brethren, and nothing but the mustache is worn. (143:372)

The shaping of the beard and mustache and the care of both were again ruled on by the Annual Meeting of 1893, Article 5. A letter of membership from a brother was not to be accepted by a church if his beard did not comply with the rules of Annual Meeting. (91:580)

The parting of the hair on the side and the shingling of it in the back become a common practice by 1900. There was no specific ruling after this period in regard to the length of the hair or the manner in which it was to be worn. Nor was there a further ruling in regard to the shaping of the beard. Older brethren in the church usually shaved the upper lip while retaining a full length beard. (Figures 26 and 27) Only those men who were unable to raise a creditable beard were excused. Some young brethren trimmed their beards close to the face. Experimentation and personal preference resulted in considerable individuality in appearance. (Figure 28) Other young brethren shaved off their beards, despite church rulings.

The overall decision regarding dress in 1911 contained this statement regarding the beard. Article 3, Section 2 read, "That the brethren wear their hair and beard in a plain and sanitary manner. That the mustache alone is forbidden." (80:5) All members were to follow this decision, which was considered to be in accordance with scripture and the will of the Holy Spirit. Ministering brethren adhered more closely to the ruling than laymen. Laymen were permitted greater leniency, or at least they took it. (Figure 29)

By 1925 the issue of the wearing of a beard

Figure 22. Shorter Hair Style, D. L. Miller, 1868.

Figure 23. Hair Style, Galen B. Royer, 1885.

Figure 24. Hair Style, H.B. Brumbaugh (1836-1919).

Figure 25. Full Beard, Galen B. Royer, c. 1905.

Figure 26. Full Beard, Frank Hay, c. 1920.

Figure 27. Trimmed Beard, Frederick Rohrer.

Figure 28. Trimmed Beard and Mustache, E.M. Crouch, 1910.

Figure 29. Clean Shaven, Roy Mohler, 1919.

came before Annual Meeting because the rules were inconsistent with the practice of the membership. Even some ministering brethren in the church had not worn a beard for some time. Many persons had joined the church who did not comply with the rule. The answer to the query, recorded as Article 25, stated:

> Inasmuch as the New Testament is silent on the question of the wearing of the beard, we decide that the wearing of the beard shall not be made a requirement for ordination to the eldership. (89:15)

The scriptural authority cited as requiring the wearing of a beard was taken from the Old Testament. The Brethren believed that the New Testament was to take precedence over the Old Testament. Without scriptural authority, the governing body could no longer prescribe the wearing of a beard. Tradition was all that demanded it. Any member whose conscience compelled him to continue to wear a beard could do so. One whose conscience did not require it was granted liberty. A very few older brethren were observed following the custom in 1970.

The rules of the church were adjusted to coincide with what had become the common practice of a large percent of the membership. The hair style was no longer an identifying characteristic of a brother in the church. Without a beard other symbols were needed to identify a brother as a member of the church. A few brethren began to wear the mustache alone, a practice still frowned upon.

The symbolic meaning of the beard has changed in at least one local church. One minister, ordinarily clean shaven, raised a beard to participate in a centennial celebration in 1970. He was accepted at the Annual Meeting, but was not accepted by members of his family when he returned to his former community. (206) To them a beard was symbolic of a person who endorsed the views of a radical. These views they could not accept as Brethren. In other churches a few young men have adopted beards and have been accepted, or at least tolerated. Two young brethren admitted to the author that their motives for wearing a beard were for reasons other than to perpetuate Brethren tradition. (206)

Hats. The broad-brimmed, black felt hat was the most distinctive part of a brother's garb. It was in contrast to the top hat, the derby, the boater, and fedora worn by fashionable gentleman during the nineteenth and twentieth centuries. The brim was flat and not cocked; the crown was without indentation. It was set straight on the head as shown in Figure 30.

Broad-brimmed hats were hung on wooden pegs or hooks placed on the walls of the meeting houses. Also they were hung on wooden pegs inserted into a board suspended over the aisle, as described for the previous century. In some churches several strands of wire over the center aisle served this same purpose. (56:181)

Leaders in the church were expected to adopt the order of dress of the Brethren and thus wear this particular hat style. Early in the nineteenth century, at least one instance was recorded of assistance being given to a young minister to adopt the proper head covering.

> Bro. Nead's dress was more stylish than was the custom of the Brethren. One feature of his attire, offensive to the Brethren, was a tall, white hat, after the style of the clergy in those days. Bro. Nead was so earnest in his work, and enjoyed his church relationship so much that they were slow to ask him to put the hat away. Finally old Bro. Benjamin Bowman decided that he could remove that hat without offending Bro. Nead. So, one Sunday, after the close of the preaching services at his own house, he asked Bro. Nead to take a walk with him. Entering the barn, he closed the door... approached a fanning mill. Reaching into the mill, he drew out a new low-crowned hat, and said, "Bro. Peter, the Brethren feel that the hat you wear is not in harmony with the humble profession you have made. We love you, and desire that you may do

Figure 30. Broad-Brimmed Hat, H.W. Strickler, c. 1913.

Figure 31. Higher Crowned Hat of Dennis Rupel, 1914.

Figure 32. Hat With Brim Rolled, David Deardorff, c. 1915.

Figure 33. Black Felt Hat, Reuel Prichett, 1969.

a great deal of good in the church." ...He took the hat and never wore any other kind of hat as long as he lived. The manner in which Bro. Bowman approached him, had such an effect upon him that he changed all his clothing and came in the full order of the church. (154:27+)

Apparently by mid-nineteenth century this style hat had become so distinctive to the brethren that other forms of headdress were not acceptable. Permission to wear fur or cloth caps was not granted by the Annual meeting of 1849, Article 3. (90:132) Reconsideration of this article came before the delegate body again in 1887. A request for wearing caps in case of necessity was granted under Article 9. (91:467) The next year Annual Meeting was petitioned to define "necessity". The answer under Article 12 stated, "We do not presume to define cases of necessity, but when worn for comfort we see no impropriety." (91:481) Furthermore, forbearance of those members of differing opinion was strongly urged.

Broad-brimmed hats were not always available in local stores unless the storekeeper took a special interest in stocking them. Enterprising entrepreneurs produced these hats especially for the plain people. An undated letter written by M. Auge of Norristown, Pennsylvania, stated that he had commenced to manufacture hats. In a second letter written in 1884, he offered stiff, semi-soft, and soft-plain hats, such as the Brethren wore, in quality fur. (175) Brims were available in widths varying from two and seven-eights to three and three-quarters inches. Crowns were either four and one-half or five inches deep. Prices ranged from $1.75 to $3.00. A twenty-five cent commission was to be given to the proprietor of the store for each hat he sold. (176)

Perceptible changes in the proportions were observed in the majority of hats worn after 1890. The brim became narrower and took on a slight roll. The crown increased in height and became slightly rounded. These alterations gave a much different appearance to the hat. Nevertheless the

hat still differed from that of the world, but it no longer was a peace symbol. Each hat took on the individual touch of its owner. (Figures 31 through 33) The Sunday hat shown in Figure 31 was preserved because it has not been the custom to bury the hat with a deceased brother. Old Sunday hats were worn out in the fields, but some men preferred caps and straw hats for daily wear. After 1920 some brethren laid aside their black felt hats for a Panama straw for summer wear on Sunday. Other brethren adopted the fedora and other fashionable styles. Therefore these brethren could not be identified by their hats as members of the church.

Two stores which sell plain hats were visited by the author in 1968. (211, 213) Hat prices were under ten dollars. The brother of each religious sect knows which one is worn by his group when making a selection from the many styles offered for sale. The situation becomes confusing to the outsider trying to discriminate between the relatively minute differences.

Coats. The suit coat of the brethren signified membership in this religious group and was symbolic of its beliefs. Ministering brethren and lay members wore coats of the same style, signifying equality of status and the priesthood of each believer. The coat was worn for all religious and social occasions, but not for daily work. Of the Sunday clothing the coat was the most costly to produce and held in the highest esteem.

Apparently the Brethren wore the cutback long coat with standing collar early in the nineteenth century. Illustrations in Nead's *Theological Writings* show this coat with trousers, rather than breeches. The front of the coat can be seen in Figure 34.

The brethren were reminded by the Annual Meeting of 1847, Article 9, that they were to be consistent in their witness. They were not to have two suits of clothes, one "in the order" for church meetings and another in the fashion of the world. (90:120) Some brethren wore the

46

Figure 34. Cutback Coat With Standing Collar, c. 1850.

Figure 35. Brethren Coat, *Scribner's Magazine*, 1901.

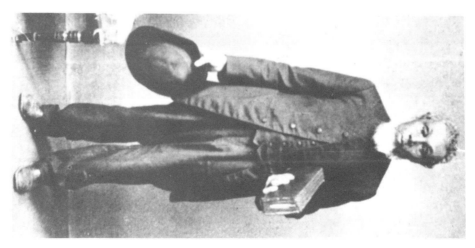

Figure 36. Brethren Coat, Elder James May.

Prince Albert or frock coat with rolled collar and lapels. These "fashionable brethren" were criticized in 1866 in Article 27 for wearing "frock and sack coats, dusters and shawls". (90:313) Offending members were to be admonished "again and again". If they did not heed they were to be dealt with according to Matthew 18.

A query came before the Annual Meeting of 1876 specifically asking whether the coat was to have a rolling or standing collar. The answer given in Article 11 was a bit evasive. (90:416) A definite decision was made the next year. The following is quoted from Article 9:

> We petition Annual Meeting to reconsider Article 11, of 1876, and so amend its answer that it make the standing collar on the coat the old order as recognized by the Brethren.
> Answer: This Annual Meeting reconsiders the above article and grants the request. (91:347)

Now there was no doubt as to what type collar was to be worn on the coat. The rest of the coat was left subject to the trends of fashion. The cutaway frock coat with standing collar became the "official Brethren coat". Both ministering and lay brethren were expected to wear this style coat. (Figure 35) A coat with slightly less rounding of the skirt was worn about 1890 and is shown in Figure 36.

The question arose as to how long the standing collar had been worn on the coat. An answer was recorded in the *Full Report* during the discussion of Article 9 of the minutes of the Annual Meeting of 1877. The moderator of the meeting said:

> As you are talking about the old order, I happened to be connected through my family, with the old brethren. More than 90 years ago my grandfather stood before the people to preach the same doctrines I preach, in identically the same cut of coat that I wear. That I know, since I knew him... that as we were similar not alone in tastes but

in our forms also, my father, when my grandfather died wore out his coat, and when my father died in 1850 I wore out his coat.... Our old fathers in our country were the same order yet but the old brethren of whom mention has been made as wearing a different collar must have come from other families not in the church. (61:28)

Men's dress coats were no longer made in the home during the last half of the nineteenth century. Brethren who wished to dress in the order of the church found that this requirement presented special problems. Some brethren ordered fabric and took it to a local tailor to be made into a suit of clothes with the proper cut. (178) One elder was known to have driven his horse and buggy forty miles to secure a suit of the correct style. (203) Enterprising entrepreneurs offered on order plain coats in addition to fashionable ones. Representatives from manufacturing firms made their selections available at Annual Meetings. Also brethren could order plain coats by mail from catalogs sent free on request. These catalogs were swatched for making fabric selections. A tape measure was provided for taking measurements. Satisfaction was guaranteed, although not always realized. Advertisements appeared in Brethren publications. The contrast between the established Brethren coat and the fashionable coat of 1903 is shown in an advertisement taken from a *Brethren Family Almanac*. (107:2) (Figure 37)

The securing of a prescribed coat was especially difficult for brethren in sparsely settled territories. Some local tailors were hesitant to make such a coat. In 1880 a Brother Price from Ohio wrote to Abraham Cassel at Harleysville, Pennsylvania. Apparently they had seen each other at a recent Annual Meeting.

> Abm, I was much smitten with your nice coat you wore here. I wish I could get a pattern of that cut, no tailor here can cut a plain coat. I am sorry I did not bring a pattern with me. (180)

WHEN YOU
WANT . . . . CLOTHING

Send to

Larimer
Manufacturing
Company.

They have been serving our
people with good goods at
moderate prices, and

Satisfaction Guaranteed

Or money refunded.

Figure 37. Advertisement for Fraternal Clothing Contrasting Brethren and Fashionable Men's Dress, 1903.

Figure 38. Adapted Clerical Collar, Edmund Book, c. 1866.

Figure 39. Brethren Hymnal in Back Coat Pocket.

Price further complained that plain coats were not worn by the brethren in Ohio. Only four brothers wore a kind of "crippled" plain coat which he refused to wear.

Perhaps all that some brethren could do to dress in the prescribed coat was to buy a fashionable coat and have the rolled collar adapted. The coat shown in Figure 38 shows evidence of being "made over". There is too much space between the end of the collar and the front corner of the coat. The collar remained turned down rather than having been altered into a standing collar. This alteration is very difficult to perform, and probably beyond the usual skills of the seamstress in the home.

Fashionable coats featured buttons for closures and for decorative purposes. The number of buttons on a Brethren coat was limited to those needed to close the front of the coat. The waistline seam of a frock coat extended from the front of the coat to the back, stopping at the juncture with the center back panels. It was the custom to place a button at this point which headed the pleats in the back of the skirt. Hip buttons on a coat were considered unnecessary by the credentials committee at one Annual Meeting. Upon its request one elder returned to his place of lodging to cut them off. His wife retorted that this request was being too strict for her. (230) Coats of this style featured a split skirt to facilitate horse back riding. The skirt lining in the back contained a pocket large enough to carry a small Bible or a Brethren hymnal of the day. (Figure 39)

Coats worn after 1900 are shown in Figures 40 through 43. Less rounding of the corner of the front of the skirt was noted in Figure 40. The back of the coat, shown in Figure 41, retained the same cut of coats worn throughout the nineteenth century. The frock coat with square front corner was worn by a few brethren after 1950. (22:5) (Figure 42) The colors of coats were conservative. Most of the elders who appeared on Standing Committee wore dark

suits. Black was the usual color, though older men sometimes wore gray. Once in a while a brother would wear a dark navy blue coat, but nothing would be said openly about it. (201)

A query concerning the cut of the prescribed coat came before the Annual Meeting of 1893. The question was asked whether the clergyman's coat or square skirted coat of that day was "in order". The discussion recorded regarding this query described this coat as being a sack coat with a clerical collar. (65:68) A negative answer was given to this query, listed as Article 9 (91:582), and to a similar query in 1903. (112:74) The dress decision of 1911 stated in Article 3, Section 1, "That the brethren wear plain clothing. The coat with the standing collar be worn, especially by the ministers and deacons." (80:5) Nothing was specified regarding the cut of the remainder of the coat.

Criticism came to those who laid aside the official frock coat which had been the order of the church. The date of change from the frock coat to the sack coat varied with the individual and the locale, perhaps over the twenty year period between 1910 and 1930. The length of these coats varied, some reaching the knee or slightly below. At first the sack coat with a clerical or standing collar featured no exterior pockets. (201) (Figure 43) Later outside pockets with flaps were accepted. Then the collar became the only identifying feature of this Brethren coat.

The three coats shown in Figures 44 through 46 were available for photographing. A cutaway frock coat with clerical collar is shown in Figures 44A and 44B. A frock coat with standing collar and less rounding of the skirt is shown in Figure 45. A shorter sack coat with exterior pockets is shown in Figure 46. The standing collar is the only feature designating this one as a Brethren coat.

All ministering brethren were expected to wear the clerical coat while performing the duties of office. Following Christ's example, the coat is removed before performing the feetwashing ser-

50

Figure 40. Frock Coat, Peter Thomas, c. 1913.

Figure 41. Frock Coat of Levi Hoover, c. 1929.

Figure 42. Frock Coat, J. Edson Ulery, c. 1930.

Figure 43. Sack Coat, Edgar Detwiler, c. 1920.

Figure 44A. Cutaway Clerical Frock Coat.

Figure 44B. Back View Without Hip Buttons.

Figure 45. Frock Coat With Square Skirt.

Figure 46. Sack Coat With Clerical Collar.

vice. Also the rite of baptism is administered without a coat. (Figure 47) If temperatures became unbearable the custom of retaining the coat might be expected. Some ministers removed their coats and preached in their shirtsleeves. Others thought this behavior inappropriate and "sweated it out". Instead of the standing collar on the sack coat, a few brethren wore a coat with a narrow round collar which had square corners. The front of the coat was buttoned to the neck. Figure 48 shows a coat of this type. This particular collar was acceptable because it was not like collars on fashionable coats. All pictures located showing coats with this style collar were of brethren connected with Brethren colleges. Therefore it may have been an idiosyncracy of college men.

After 1910 some ministering brethren chose to wear the clerical vest with a business suit instead of the sack coat with clerical collar. Thus the clerical collar was retained as a symbol of the cleric to the member and nonmember. (see Figure 49) A clerical vest was advantageous for two reasons. A fashionable suit could be purchased without having to pay for a custom tailored collar. A "plain" vest could be added at little expense. Since the vest did not need to be replaced as often as the suit, it did not wear out as quickly as the suit. Furthermore, the suit could be worn without the vest and thus without the standing collar. The clerical vest was adopted in Pennsylvania after 1945, although earlier in other states. It too is gradually being laid aside. (195) The lay brother and the majority of the ministering brethren have adopted the three-piece business suit with rolling collar on the coat. Therefore it is not possible to identify these brethren as members of the church by their coats.

In 1968 suits in clerical styles were available on order at stores offering plain clothing for various religious groups. Brethren were able to purchase a sack coat with clerical collar, matching vest, and trousers. Prices were in the current range for such tailored garments. Measurements for the suit were taken at the store. The style and fabric selections were made there also. The fabrics offered for sale were of excellent quality, with some being imports. Colors varied from black to light gray or navy, in solid or tweed effects. (Figure 50) The measurements and fabric were sent to a manufacturing firm for men's wear. The tailor at one store did only alterations. At a customer's request he would change a wide lapelled fashionable coat with turned down collar to a coat with a standing collar. However, the narrow lapelled fashionable coats of the 1960's were too difficult to alter. (192)

Other Items of Apparel. The remainder of the outer clothing worn by the brethren was not prescribed and therefore differed very little from that worn by men in general. No rulings were found in the minutes of the Annual Meetings for the nineteenth and twentieth centuries regarding trousers, shirts, overcoats, boots, and shoes. Only ostentation with regard to these items was objectionable. Conservative selections were made in order that these items might be in agreement in line, color, and texture with the prescribed items.

Men's clothing in general became more conservative in the 1840's than that worn in any previous period of history. (33:91) The fly front had been introduced into men's trousers by this time. However, some brethren continued to wear broadfall trousers much later. Their use with cutaway coats continued for three-quarters of the nineteenth century. The legs of trousers were not creased until the end of the century. The closeness of fit and width of the cuff paralleled the fashionable trousers of each decade. Suspenders were used throughout the century.

Late in the nineteenth century a matched three-piece suit and accessories constituted a brother's good Sunday clothing. Since trousers wore out faster than coats, a brother's trousers did not always match his coat. During weekly meetings,

Figure 47. Coat Removed for Baptizing, c. 1850.

Figure 48. Round Collar on Coat, J. Henry Showalter.

Figure 49. Clerical Vest, Frank Carper, 1968.

Figure 50. "Plain" Suit Fabrics, 1968.

laymen wore everyday pants, patched or not patched, and sat on the back bench. Clean trouser cuffs were not easy to maintain in early spring when clay mud was hub deep on a buggy wheel.

The collarless shirt worn by the brethren in the nineteenth century was finished with a band at the neck. (Figure 51) The sleeves of this hand-made shirt were finished with a one-inch band and the vent closed with a button and button-hole. The shoulder area was reinforced in both front and back. Each side seam had a vent at the lower edge. The twelve-inch front opening was finished with a facing turned toward the right side and closed with three buttons and buttonholes. These early shirts did not extend beyond the collar or cuffs of the coat.

Sunday shirts were white, and many everyday shirts were too. Muslin was cheaper than other fabrics, wore better, and could be boiled on washday. Colored fabrics faded quickly under heavy laundry processes. Dyes were much improved late in the century and colored shirts became popular for daily wear.

In the 1890's the shirts worn with clerical coats had detachable collars. These collars were always white, even if the shirts were not. A colored shirt collar just was not worn with the Brethren coat. Extra shirt collars were packed in the valises of the brethren away from home for evangelistic meetings and Annual Meeting. Some ministers were known for their impeccable linens; others, for their lack of them.

Both the collar and the cuffs of these shirts were heavily starched, if not the body of the shirt. If the womenfolk could not meet their menfolk's standards in laundering collars, they were sent to a commercial launderer. (191) Stiff celluloid collars partially replaced the heavily starched cloth collars. These ever ready collars saved laundry and proved quite satisfactory until they showed aging. In time the celluloid cracked, peeled, and yellowed. Usually they were disposed of by burning. After 1950 collars of plasticized fabrics replaced the earlier celluloid

ones. The shirt shown in Figure 52 was available in 1968. It required the plasticized collar shown in Figure 53 and cuff links for the French cuffs.

All of the detachable collars worn by the brethren opened in the front. They should not be confused with other clerical styles which open in the back and which were not worn by the brethren. Detachable collars were attached to the shirt with studs inserted through buttonholes, one at center back and one at center front. (Figure 54) Some studs were made of ivory; others were made of gold or silver alloys. (Figure 55). In readiness for Sunday morning, an alert wife inserted these studs after ironing the shirt and collar.

Few shirts were made at home after 1900. No longer could the home seamstress compete with the nation's garment industry. Fabrics selected were the usual cotton shirtings found on the market of the day. Shirts with collars attached came into fashion during the second decade of the twentieth century and were accepted by many of the brethren. Although a variety of sizes were available, some men found it necessary to adjust the length of the sleeve of a bought shirt with sleeve holders, often a band of black elastic. After 1920 shirts with soft collars became popular and no longer required the heavy starching previously considered necessary. Gradually shirts with rounded collars were exchanged for shirts with pointed collars. These shirts were worn with both the Brethren coat and the clerical vest.

Overcoats were without religious significance. A myth exists among the brethren that one should not go to Annual Meeting without an overcoat. Early in the nineteenth century some brethren wore a caped overcoat. There was a collar in addition to the cape, and the skirt was very long. (Figure 56) Elder John Kline gave this description of an overcoat worn on his trip to Pennsylvania in 1837.

Figure 51. White Shirt With Neckband, c. 1890.

Figure 52. Shirt With Neckband and French Cuffs, 1968.

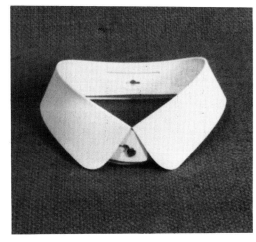

Figure 53. Fused Detachable Shirt Collar, 1968.

Figure 54. Collar Stud, Jonathan Cripe, c. 1905.

Figure 55. Shirt Collar Studs.

Figure 56. Caped Overcoat, *Harper's Magazine*, 1889.

Figure 57. Overcoat, Samuel Ober, 1942.

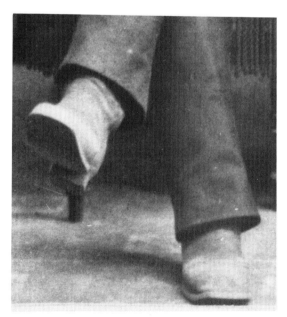

Figure 58. Boots of Jonathon Cripe, 1876.

Figure 59. Shoes, *Scribner's Magazine*, 1901.

The order of dress for the traveler consisted of a great coat, made of heavy, compact stuff, with long skirt reaching to the feet, and a large cape attached, covering completely the shoulders and buttoning over the breast, constituting a covering defying both rain and storm... Every saddle of the day was provided with what was called a coat-pad, fastened to the saddle just behind the seat and furnished with straps and buckles so as to hold an overcoat, when properly rolled up and fastened in perfect order whilst traveling. (168:9)

The wearing of military clothing became an issue during the Civil War. Article 10 of the minutes of Annual Meeting of 1864 asked what should be done with a brother who wore a soldier's overcoat in the pulpit. The answer was that he should be admonished, and, if persistent, he should be dealt with according to Matthew 18. (90:280) Furthermore, the wearing of military clothing at anytime was without sanction because of the beliefs the Brethren held against war. Overcoats without capes were worn at the end of the nineteenth century and during the twentieth century. The overcoat shown in Figure 57 was worn in 1942.

The type and condition of the soil made a difference in the kind of boots worn. Leather and felt boots were popular in the nineteenth century. The latter were seldom worn to church. Boots were tall enough to reach well above the ankle, as shown in Figure 58. Spring thawing resulted in soft mud at every doorstep. A device called a boot jack was a part of the accoutrements at the back door of a rural home. One foot held down this wooden device while the heel of the boot on the other foot was caught in the notched front end to remove it. Boots were not removed during church services, which necessitated scrubbing of the wooden floors of the church in late spring.

In the early part of the nineteenth century shoes were made in the home by a family member, or an itinerant who plied the trade. Shoes of this type are shown in Figure 59. Shoes which

had the sole stitched to the upper part by means of a sewing machine were available after the Civil War. (49:7435) Even though the number of bought shoes increased, shoe repair continued at home well into the twentieth century. Since no specific footwear was prescribed by the church, commercially made shoes in conservative styles were bought at the local dry goods store. Usually black shoes were selected, because they were appropriate with a gray, black, or dark navy blue suit. Dress shoes were of two types, oxfords and the laced shoe which covered the ankle. Often during inclement weather both dress and work shoes were covered with artics or rubbers.

Handkerchiefs, mufflers, mittens, or gloves were a part of a brother's attire. For the most part they were commercially made after 1900. Older men were often seen carrying a simple cane with curved handle. All members of a family used the large black umbrella, often featuring a cane-like handle.

Neckties. To the Brethren a necktie symbolized a fashionable man who held beliefs incongruent with the Brethren way of life. However, at the end of the nineteenth century, a few brethren with more liberal views wore a soft black tie with their Brethren coats. (Figure 60) The question of wearing fashionable neckties was brought before the Annual Meeting of 1899. Article 7 read:

> We the members of the North Manchester church, ask Annual Meeting through District Meeting to define what is meant by the term fashionable neckties!
> Answer by District Meeting: The term "fashionable", as applied to neckties in the committee's report referred to, signifies all neckties except those worn for comfort or health.
> Answer: Passed by Annual Meeting. (91:698)

The differences between a fashionable necktie worn as a status symbol and a muffler to protect the neck in cold weather was obvious to most

Figure 60. Soft Black Necktie, J.B. Brumbaugh.

Figure 61. Without Necktie, Fred Replogle, c. 1910.

Figure 62. Bow Tie, David Weaver, c. 1915.

Figure 63. Four-in-Hand Tie, Ora Burroughs, c. 1918.

brethren.

The necktie was the most contested single item of apparel worn by the brethren in the first quarter of the twentieth century. Changes in the occupations that the brethren now followed demanded a change in dress. With the adoption of more items of fashionable dress, it was logical that the necktie should be added as the final touch. Some brethren contended that a necktie was needed to maintain their new positions, whereas others worked at their jobs without a tie even though they wore a lapelled coat. (Figure 61)

The dress decision of 1911 did not give a specific ruling regarding the necktie. In 1912 a query was sent to Annual Meeting requesting a settlement of the disturbances caused by inconsistencies between those congregations which permitted the wearing of the necktie and those which did not. The answer proposed by Standing Committee read as follows; "We require that our ministers and deacons refrain from wearing neckties and strongly advise against any of our members wearing them." (72:185) A substitute motion was adopted which returned this paper to the congregation which presented it. During the debate one member expressed the sentiments of many by contending that the necktie was a symbol of worldly fashions and that this growing evil of adopting fashionable dress must be stopped. Logic follows that the necktie was considered an instrument of the devil. Another member questioned whether the necktie was an ornament or a piece of clothing. Once this was decided, the decision whether to wear or not to wear a necktie was simple to make. A third member questioned whether a plain necktie was acceptable and only a fancy one was to be rejected. Other members were grieved that such a query should come before the meeting after the previous year's decision on the dress question in general. (111:380)

In 1915 the Quinter church petitioned Annual Meeting to say whether the dress decision of 1911 "forbid the wearing of the fashionable necktie". Some members opposed the query because of the necessity to define the term "fashionable necktie". Article 5 read as follows:

> The letter of the dress decision of 1911 does not forbid the wearing of the necktie, but we urgently advise our brethren to refrain from wearing neckties and other unnecessary articles of adornment. (83:11)

After 1919 the wearing of neckties was no longer debated as a specific item of business at the national level.

In 1920, a report entitled "Difference of Practice and Teaching" was brought before Annual Meeting. Section 6 of the adopted report stated:

> We discourage the wearing of neckties, but we decide that the wearing of the necktie should not be made a test of membership or fellowship. (86:12)

Practice did differ from the teachings of the church. (Figure 62) One minister was asked to lay aside his tie before he was ordained as an elder. (195) He does not wear a necktie today because he has continued to wear the sack coat with clerical collar. A delegate to Annual Meeting in this decade was asked by the credentials committee to remove his necktie. (206) One brother was informed by two solicitous deacons that he was ineligible for a church letter to take to the host church at college because be wore a necktie. (206)

The four-in-hand tie became fashionable by 1900. A few young brethren adopted it while others waited twenty years. (Figure 63) In 1928, one elder bought a tie to wear with camping clothes, although he never wore it with his clerical coat. (22:42) Thus he differentiated between what was appropriate for him to wear with a Brethren coat for church activities and clothing for other activities.

With the laying aside of the Brethren coat with its clerical collar for a lapelled coat and a necktie, a brother could no longer be distinguished in appearance from a man of the world. His changes in dress had been completed and denoted that the walls of isolation had been broken down and he was interacting with the world at large. A reversal of this trend has been cited in one instance. The moderator of the Annual Meeting for 1972 wrote that he has decided not to wear a necktie during his year in office. His motives were to express his Christian freedom in a culture requiring conformity to middle class values and to identify both with his Brethren heritage and with today's Brethren youth rejecting present day conformity. (118:20+)

Gold. The Brethren believed that two verses of the Bible forbade the wearing of gold, I Timothy 2:9 and I Peter 3:3. In the minutes of Annual Meeting for 1864, Article 7, the question arose whether the carrying of a gold watch was included in the restrictions of the above verses. The answer was that the carrying of a gold watch might lead to pride and therefore was prohibited. (90:280) Further discussion about gold did not come before Annual Meeting until 1889. Article 2 asked if the carrying of a gold watch was of sufficient cause to expel a member from the church. The decision, recorded in the *Full Report*, said that it was sufficient. (64:23+) The Annual Meeting of 1891 in Article 19-1/2 stated that the wearing of gold in any form violated the scriptures and therefore it could not be tolerated. (163:490) No mention was made concerning the use of gold for dental restoration, a common practice before 1900.

The Reading Church requested the Annual Meeting of 1910 to redefine her position on gold in order to overcome inconsistencies found among members in various churches. (113:286) The answer prepared by Standing Committee and adopted by the delegate body referred the gold question to the committee studying the dress question in its totality. The dress decision of 1911 stated in Article 3, Section 5, "That gold

for ornament, and jewelry of all kinds, shall not be worn." (80:5)

At the end of the nineteenth century some brethren carried pocket watches with silver cases. More brethren did so early in the twentieth century. The use of silver for such purposes was acceptable. (Figure 64) The display of a gold watch chain was considered worldly. Either a silver chain, a black silk cord, or leather strap was considered more appropriate. (Figure 65) Gold spectacle frames were more satisfactory than brass. Brass frames left greenish-black marks on temples moistened with perspiration. Silver frames were permitted. (Figure 66) Razors with plain handles and simple cases were to be preferred over more elaborate ones. (Figure 67)

Advertisements for selling spectacles and watches appeared regularly in *The Gospel Messenger* in 1898. However, the Annual Meeting of 1899 stated in Article 11 that all advertising should be discontinued from the official church paper. (91:811) Therefore the agent was forced to distribute a special leaflet advertising cut-rate prices on items he had in stock. According to the leaflet these watches had nickel cases although the works included settings of rubies and gold. (102)

The Annual Meeting of 1905 received two queries concerning the selling of certain items of merchandise by Brethren merchants as inconsistent with previous decisions. (91:811) The committee's report in 1906 stated that it was wrong for brethren to sell "playing cards, dice, diamonds, gold rings, gold watches and other items of display." (84:25) In the face of members' further encroachment on the rulings of Annual Meeting concerning the wearing of jewelry, the elders of the District of Eastern Pennsylvania, in 1920, resolved to abide by the decision of the Annual Meeting of 1911. (149:569)

Marriages were performed without the ring ceremony in the nineteenth century and the first quarter of the twentieth century. The increased

Figure 64. Pocket Watch, c. 1900.

Figure 66. Spectacles of Peter Keyser.

Figure 65. Watch Chain, Elijah Umble, after 1866.

Figure 67. Straight Razor and Case, c. 1900.

use of rings caused the White Oak Congregation in eastern Pennsylvania to vote in 1944 that ministers who performed weddings with the ring ceremony were not acting consistently with the teachings of the New Testament. (93:4) By 1970 the wearing of wedding rings was a common practice across the Brotherhood.

Graveclothes. The custom in the early part of the nineteenth century was to wrap the deceased in a winding sheet. Apparently one was kept in readiness in the home. Anna Bowman related that her father came for the winding sheet upon hearing that Elder John Kline had been shot from ambush during the Civil War. (168:18) A white shroud replaced the winding sheet and its use continued even after 1900. It was customary for the undertaker to furnish a shroud upon request. Therefore items of clothing left by the deceased were available for use by other members of the immediate family.

The church did not dictate the color for clothing. Social custom decreed black as the color for clothing for funeral occasions and periods of mourning. The uncertainty of life caused preparations to be made in the event of these occasions. Usually only one set of dress garments was available at a time. They were often black, in readiness, should such an occasion occur.

Members attending funerals were to have respect for the gravity of the occasion. The wearing of extravagant dress was considered to be an "abomination in the sight of God", according to the minutes of the Annual Meeting of 1819, Article 5. Furthermore the "body of Christ" was not to follow after the "body of the world". (90:56)

Hair and Clothing Styles Worn by the Sisters

The hair and clothing styles worn by the sisters during the nineteenth century and early twentieth century identified them as belonging to a particular religious group. The most significant item, the cap, had both religious and social significance. Other items were selected on the basis of the ideal of nonconformity to the fashions of the world. Individual and regional differences were evident. Changes were noted despite the rulings of Annual Meeting which favored the retention of one mode of dress.

Discussion has been limited to a descriptive analysis of the outer garments worn, their significance, rulings in regard to them, and brief comparisons with fashionable items. The illustrations shown in Figures 68 through 179 reflect the dress worn during the last half of the nineteenth century and the first three-quarters of the twentieth century.

Hair. Long hair was worn by the sisters throughout the nineteenth century and for the first quarter of the twentieth century. Even fashion had not decreed that a woman cut her hair. During this time the character of the few women who did cut their hair was regarded with suspicion. (199) A sister considered her long hair to be her crowning glory, as stated in I Corinthians 11. If she cut her hair, she brought shame upon herself, according to this scripture. It was sinful on two accounts: she disposed of the glory that God had given her and she imitated the opposite sex. The only justification for cutting the hair was for health reasons.

No rulings concerning a sister's hair were found in the minutes of Annual Meeting before 1911. For this year, Article 3, Section 3, stated that a sister's "hair be worn in a becoming Christian manner." (80:5) The decision implied that a sister would follow the scripture just cited. The hair was not to be braided or plaited for this too was in violation of two other verses of scripture, I Timothy 2:9 and I Peter 3:3.

The hair was arranged close to the head to fit under the cap which also was required by the scripture. After 1850 the hair was smoothed down from a center part and arranged in a bun on the back of the head. A young girl in the

1860's (9:144) and 1870's sometimes arranged her hair in a chignon as shown in Figure 68. By 1890 she more often combed it straight back from the forehead before arranging it in a bun. (Figure 69)

An article in *The Gospel Messenger* for 1909 pleaded for simplicity in the dressing of the hair and warned against worldly fashions.

> Women of all ages have ornamented their hair. Today fashion requires puffing, ratting and crimping of it, with fancy side combs. The spirit of this command would forbid us dressing our hair in other than a plain, tidy manner. (156:35)

The puffing of the hair was aided by the use of rats and curling tongs heated over an oil lamp. A slight pompadour effect could be produced by combing the hair straight back in a loose manner and inserting combs. (Figures 70 and 71)

Hairpins were made of wire and later of plastic materials. (Figure 72) Combs were made of hard rubber, tortoise shell, celluloid, and also plastic materials. (Figures 73 and 74) The fancy comb shown in Figure 75 looked inappropriate under a cap and in all probability was laid aside at baptism.

A young girl often braided her long hair and let the braid fall down her back. Sometimes the end of the braid was caught up at the back of the neck. Some girls placed a large bow above the looped braid. Usually the bow was black, though some girls wore navy blue. (198) (Figure 76) Bows were also considered inappropriate when the cap was adopted. By 1920 some little girls had their hair cut to enter grade school. Thus they had to let it grow in order to join the church.

Bobbing of the hair pitted fashion against the scripture. In 1970 some of the older sisters and a few younger sisters wore long hair. The majority had cut their hair, and many had it dressed professionally. Thus the method of wearing the hair no longer identified these sisters as members of the church.

Caps. Women have veiled their heads for many centuries for two reasons. First, a veil was a symbol of marriage and set the married woman apart from the unmarried. Second, the Christian church required it, as stated in I Corinthians 11. Since the veil had both a religious and social significance, it was doubly binding that a sister wear one.

In the early nineteenth century the word "cap" was used in place of the word veil. At this time most applicants for membership in the church already were married. Therefore these sisters already had adopted the cap. Having adopted the cap of matrimony, the sisters did not find it difficult to accept this requirement of the church. Later in the century the age of applicants began to drop below that of marriage. This necessitated the adoption of the cap by the single sister. The question of wearing a covering on the head came before the Annual Meeting in 1848. Article 6 asked:

> Whether the Scriptures require that women, praying or prophesying, should have any other covering than the hair, and whether it includes alike married and unmarried women?
> Considered, unanimously, that they all should have a covering on their heads. (90:124)

Thus the single girl adopted the cap as a head covering at baptism, as required by the scriptures and the custom of the church. This set her apart from the single girl of the world and also implied that she was married. This decision was reaffirmed again in 1862, Article 19. (90:258)

The kind of head covering became the question before the Annual Meeting of 1856. The answer given to Article 26 read, "We are satisfied,... that the plain cap worn by our dear aged sisters, is a covering, as required by the Scriptures according to Paul." (117:29) The scripture was again cited as the authority for wearing a covering on the head. Since the type

Figure 68. Hair With Center Part, Malinda Weaver, c. 1870.

Figure 69. Unparted Hair, Alma Van Winkle, c. 1900.

Figure 70. Puffed Hair Style, Elsie Rupel, c. 1918.

Figure 71. Long Hair Style, Edith Rupel, 1970.

Figure 72. Hairpin.

Figure 73. Side Comb.

Figure 75. Decorative Comb, Mary Rebecca Miller, c. 1880.

Figure 74. Decorative Comb.

Figure 76. Hair Bow, Florence Rohrer, c. 1910.

to be worn followed that customarily worn by the aged sisters in the church, it left little choice for the restyling of the cap and no choice in selecting a new style.

Self-pride and a desire to emulate the fashions of the world were given in Article 27, 1866, as two reasons for sisters appearing without their caps. (90:313) Disobedient sisters were to be treated gently, yet firmly according to Article 22, 1870. (90:357) Disciplinary action was taken in many local churches. The minutes of one church in eastern Pennsylvania bear record of the action taken. "Sister Mary... upon refusing to hear the church in the wearing of apparel, especially the covering, was disowned by the church." (97)

Decisions by the official body of the church did not stop discussion. Perhaps C.H. Balsbaugh summed up the contentions concerning women's headdress in an article he wrote for *The Gospel Messenger* in 1887.

> To Philosophize, and fish up historical evidence, pro or con, only tends to bewilder, and cut the nerves and arteries of faith. To press the conventionalism of Apostolic times, as some do, to invalidate its distinctive religious character, and thus put it into the category of a nineteenth century non-essential is to place our feet in a theological quagmire. (115:370)

Despite his warnings others expressed their opinions and interpretations of I Corinthians 11. Of the many that spoke out, S. Z. Sharp gave a most lucid exegesis of the scripture in this same church paper in 1896. His interpretation favored the wearing of a head covering for the following reasons. The veil was symbolic of the relationship of woman to man, of her restoration by Christ after Eve's sin, and of her right to pray and prophesy. By wearing a cap she bore witness to the world of her redeemed status and Christ's power. (153:194) For the sister the cap was an expression of the Brethren belief in the priesthood of each believer.

The Annual Meeting of 1893 ruled in Article 11 that any minister who contended that the cap was not necessary was to be admonished and dealt with according to Matthew 18. Elders of the church were to admonish sisters who failed to wear a covering during grace at meals, as ruled by the Annual Meeting of 1893, Article 11. (91:582) The issue was again brought before the Annual Meeting of 1898. The discussion, recorded in the *Full Report*, reached a consensus that there were already adequate minutes to be followed without the addition of more. Therefore the query was returned to the district from which it came. (66:16+)

Ministers continued to preach concerning the cap and writers continued to contribute articles to church publications. Exegeses on I Corinthians 11 continued to pile up and were often repetitive. The main points were summarized by L.W. Teeter in an article printed in *The Gospel Messenger* in 1910. (164:697) The points discussed were enlarged over those presented for the previous century. The Brethren believed that a woman's status was second to that of man from the time of creation. It was she who contributed to man's fall at the time of the original sin. She could approach God only through the supplications of her husband. Christ restored her right to make supplication on her own. The head covering was symbolic of her restored status. She affirmed this right at baptism and therefore put on the cap at this time. The cap gave her the authority to pray and to prophesy in the name of Christ. If she wore it, she would be sustained in these exhortations by the ministrations of the angels.

The cap was worn under the authority of the scriptures, out of respect to the custom of the Christian church through the centuries, the rulings of Annual Meeting, and as a sign of marriage. Any attempt at its removal brought forth much heated debate. By leaving off her cap, a sister was perceived as having lost her status, her right for supplication, and the support of the spiritual universe. The sister who prayed or prophesied without it failed to recognize Christ's redeeming power, prayed in vain, and differed not from a heathen woman. By removing her cap she renounced her faith, nullified her baptism, and partook of the sacraments unworthily. Also she broke with a custom of the Christian church for over the past nineteen centuries. She no longer upheld the Brethren belief in the priesthood of each believer, nor did she proclaim this belief to the world. Furthermore, she claimed equality in status with her husband and renounced her marriage vow of being under his headship.

In many homes the daily custom of wearing the cap was neglected, even at time of family worship and grace at family meals. This fact was decried. The dress decision of 1911 restated the former position of the church in Article 3, Section 4, which read, "That the veil be worn in time of prayer and prophesying (I Cor. 11:1-16, R.V.). The plain cap is regarded as meeting the requirements of scriptural teaching on the subject." (80:5) By this time the cap came to be called a "prayer covering" or a "prayer veil". This change in name implied that the cap or covering was not worn daily but put on only during times of worship, which was true. It also implied that it no longer signified marriage.

In 1925 a query petitioned Annual Meeting "to give a plain interpretation of the doctrine of the prayer veil". (89:14) The minutes, as found in the *Full Report*, gave three reasons for making this study. The teaching of the doctrine of the prayer veil and the practice of wearing it were being neglected. A restatement of its spiritual meaning would be a good thing. A study of the scriptures and their interpretation would be wholesome. (76:139) The report presented by the committee and adopted by Annual Meeting in 1926 is summarized as follows: that a woman's head was to be covered in worship, a man's head uncovered; that a woman's hair was to be uncut, a man's hair cut; and that Paul's

teaching applied to the Christian church in its totality, not to the Corinthian church alone. (77:57) The former position of the church regarding the cap or prayer veil was reaffirmed with the acceptance of the report and this report remains unchanged. No further statement in regard to the cap has appeared in the minutes of Annual Meeting since that time.

One brave sister who wrote an article for the church paper did not enter into the discussion of the doctrinal implications of the cap. She considered the cap a holy garment and not to be made an object of admiration by adornment. It was to be made "plain", kept neat and clean, and treated with respect at all times. (163:490) The use of only white fabric symbolized purity.

The caps worn by the sisters before 1850 were illustrated in Nead's *Theological Writings*, published in that year. (Figure 77) The puffed crown allowed room for long hair to be fashioned into a bun on the back of the head. The wide frontlet framed the face closely, allowing none or only a small amount of the hair to show. The application of small strips of fabric as a finish at the edge of the frontlet and across the lower edge of the crown at the neck gave a different silhouette than the plain cap just discussed. (Figures 78 and 79) The strips edging the frontlet and neckline met at the corner and continued to form a part of the tie. (Figure 80) Sisters wearing caps of this type are shown in Figures 81 and 82.

Although the sisters were to wear "plain caps", decorative touches were observed on some. Figure 83 shows a cap edged with lace, one and one-half inches wide. The ties either were removed or else it was worn without any. Variation in the width and length of fabric or ribbon used for ties was an individual matter, although extremely wide ties were looked upon as an expression of pride and vain show. One elder admonished the sisters in his congregation for letting the ties on their caps hang freely. (97) (Figure 84) By 1900 white ties were being

Figure 77. Sisters' Plain Caps, c. 1850.

Figure 78. Edged Cap, Catharine L. Miller, c. 1870.

Figure 79. Edged Cap, Catherine H. Ullery.

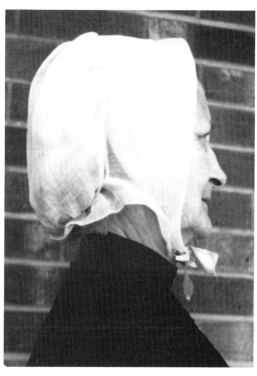

Figure 80. Plain Cap of Elizabeth Replogle (1804-1873).

Figure 81. Sisters Wearing Plain Caps, *Ladies Home Journal*, 1898.

Figure 82. Three Sisters Wearing Similar Caps Late in the Nineteenth Century.

70

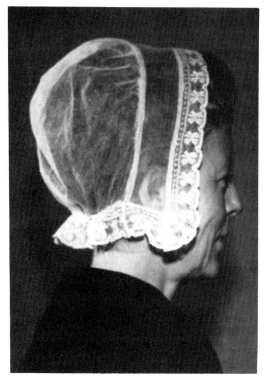

Figure 83. Lace Trimmed Cap of Elizabeth Replogle (1804-1873).

Figure 84. Decoration on Cap, Lucinda Beeghley.

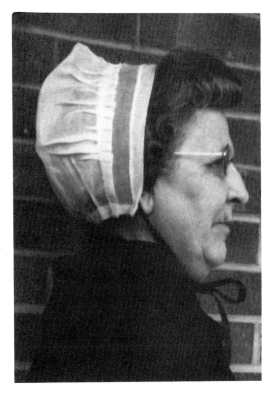

Figure 85. Cap of Susan Deardorff (1840-1922), Black Ties.

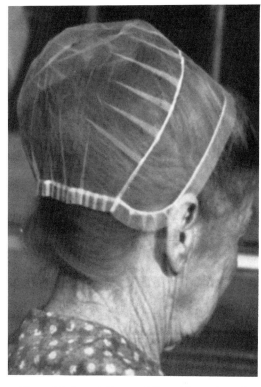

Figure 86. Round-Cornered Cap of Laura Madeira, c. 1926.

exchanged for black ones. This too was frowned upon for it was "new". (189) (Figure 85) The removal of the ties permitted the corner of the cap to stand away from the head giving a rather inartistic effect when viewed from the front.

Changes were made in the style of caps worn over the years, even though they were to be patterned after those worn "by the aged sisters". Perhaps these changes can be explained in the liberty allowed the sisters in the making of their caps, as expressed by the editor of the church paper in 1905.

> The church ought not to have to say how a prayer covering should be made. The sense of propriety, the sense of fitness, as well as the idea and spirit of sacredness ought to regulate a matter of that sort... While the letter may permit considerable variation regarding the form, suited to different ages and conditions, without in any manner interfering with the spirit. (125:601)

Caps worn during the twentieth century differed from those worn in the nineteenth. Changes noted were further reduction in size of the crown and the frontlet, or brim. A slight rounding of the front corner of the cap is shown in Figure 86. This change was commented on in a letter to the editor of *The Gospel Messenger* in 1908.

> Their bonnets were of the greatly diminished sort, while their caps had been cut down until only a semblance of the once neat and becoming prayer covering of our sisters remained... with this cutting down of distinctive parts of modest attire for saintly women, it will not be many years until that phase of nonconformity will disappear, principle, method and all. (113:362)

With further rounding of the cap, no indication of a corner remained. (Figure 87) The narrowing of the frontlet, or brim, continued until it became less than an inch wide. (Figure 88)

Upon discarding the frontlet, or brim, only the crown remained. This style of cap was called a "round prayer veil". The pattern consisted of either a circle or a slight oval. The edge of the fabric was pleated at intervals to make it conform to the shape of the head. The spacing of the pleats varied: single, double, or triple. Single pleated caps were the easiest to make and explains their popularity. The pleats were held in place by either one or two rows of machine stitching or a narrow band of folded fabric. If no band were used, the cut edge of the fabric was turned far enough under to be caught in the rows of machine stitching holding the pleats. (Figure 89) To the astonishment of other sisters, a few added a narrow strip of lace to the edge of their round caps. Round caps continued to diminish in size. In 1968 a teen-age sister was observed wearing a cap of very small diameter over her long tresses. (Figure 90) A question arose in the mind of a more conservative sister whether a cap of this size fulfilled the scriptural requirement of a veiled head. (206) Cap styles observed by the author while visiting churches during 1968 through 1970 are shown in Figures 87 through 90.

All caps were handmade with great expertise on the part of the seamstress. The handling of sheer fabrics, the folding of narrow hems, and the even spacing of fine pleats called for great skill. Some sisters who became very adept in making caps made them for others for a nominal fee. After Ladies Aid Societies were organized, they became responsible for making the caps and offered them for sale. Not everybody in the society had the skill or cared to make them. Usually cap making was left to those with deft fingers. One sister was placed in charge of selling them. The profit was minimal, but a source of ready-made caps was appreciated by the less skilled. In many churches the society gave a cap free to each new sister at baptism.

The patterns for caps were passed from one seamstress to another, from one local church to another, and from one state to another. Innovations resulted in a wide variation of the basic style, but the major change was the

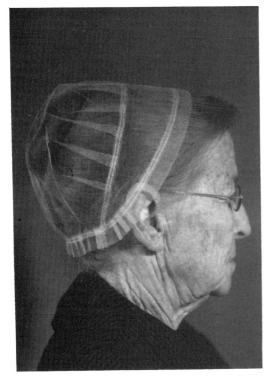

Figure 87. Two-Piece Cap of Mary Geiger, c. 1916.

Figure 88. Two-Piece Cap, Ella Carper, 1967.

Figure 89. One-Piece Cap, Fannie Stambaugh, 1970.

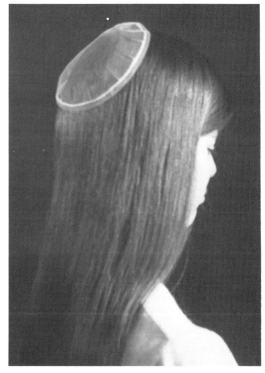

Figure 90. Cap Worn by a Teen-Age Sister, 1968.

reduction in size. This change was commented upon by the editor of the church paper.

> We do not know who introduced the style, but we do know that the caps were largely advertised, and sent far and wide through the mails. They are still being made and in time may find their way into all parts of the Brotherhood.
>
> On reading reports from our aid societies, it will be observed that these societies make and dispose of a number of prayer coverings. If they will persist in making only the kind of coverings becoming sisters, who mean to conform to the instructions of Paul in I Cor. 11, they can, in a large measure, help counteracting the influence of those who would have the small coverings become more general. The influence must be counteracted, or the neat prayer covering, so becoming devout women, will soon be a thing of the past. (147:122)

Fabrics used for caps in the nineteenth century were fine grades of linen or cotton. An advertisement in the *Brethren Almanac* for 1902 gave a list of fabrics available on order: tarlatan, bobbinette, chiffon, and Swiss cottons. Silk net was used also. Prospective customers could ask for free samples from enterprising members who kept cap fabrics in stock. Discounts were given to Ladies Aid Societies. (108:54) Cotton thread in sizes 70 to 100 was considered best for stitching the sheer fabrics on the sewing machine.

The fragility of the caps necessitated their being laundered separately from the family wash. They were hand washed, starched, and ironed as the fabric required. From the entries in one sister's diary it appeared that she wore a cap per week before refurbishing it. (169)

Silk net was very difficult to launder satisfactorily. Some sisters tried home drycleaning methods with only fair success and at great danger. The naptha or gasoline partially removed the soil from the silk, but very little from the tightly twisted cotton thread. Badly soiled caps were disposed of by burning.

All caps available for purchase in 1968 at the Marian and Ruth Shop in Mount Joy, Pennsylvania, were made of nylon fabric. The cost was one dollar or less. They were mailed on request if the customer knew the size and style she wanted. Over one hundred sizes of two-piece style caps were in stock in 1968. (219) Since these caps were made of nylon, they were very washable and outlasted caps made of other fabrics.

After 1900 some sisters no longer wore the cap continuously. There was need for storing the cap in some readily available place. The dresser drawer in the bedroom, or the cupboard in the kitchen, or the pocket on the apron served the purpose. If the cap was worn only for church services, it was folded and slipped between the pages of a sister's Bible or into her handbag. Upon arrival at church, the protective head covering was replaced by the cap. This practice resulted in shelves and small mirrors being placed inside the entrance of the church. It also meant that a sister's male partner had to hesitate in the vestibule while she put on her cap. This slight pause slowed traffic and caused embarrassment to guests unaware of the practice.

If the cap was worn continually, it was removed while doing certain work activities. The daily chore of milking cows presented the possibility of losing one's cap when the cow was trying to chase a persistent fly with her tail. Either the cap was removed for such tasks or a protective head covering was placed over it. (187) Girls enrolled in physical education classes in school had to make a decision regarding their caps. The usual practice has been to remove them during periods of activity.

The cap was to be worn when attending union services with other religious bodies. If the other religious group also required a cap, a sister felt much at ease. In churches which permitted fashionable hats, a sister often felt conspicuous wearing her cap. Sometimes she compromised by leaving on her bonnet which covered her cap.

Occasions for which the cap is worn can be arranged in a hierarchy. The most solemn occasions were the ordination of a sister or her husband into the ministry, the dedication of a sister to full time Christian service at Annual Meeting, or the marriage ceremony. The communion service, the Sunday morning church service, other church services, family worship, grace at meals, and continuous daily wear completed the rank. In this hierarchy, if a sister wore her cap for one occasion, she wore it for all the occasions preceding it in the rank. Because of its significance, the cap was the last item of plain dress to be retained by a sister when changing to more fashionable dress. When she removed her cap, she removed the last vestige of the garb which historically had identified a sister as a member of the church.

While visiting local churches during 1968 through 1970, this investigator observed that in some churches not one sister wore a cap; in other churches almost all of the sisters wore caps. More elderly sisters than young sisters wore caps. More officiary sisters than lay sisters wore caps. A possibility exists that the cap may be used by observers as an index to the degree of conservatism of an individual or of a local church congregation. Also the reduction in size may reflect a reduction in its significance.

Bonnets. The wearing of a head covering out-of-doors has been a time honored custom. The bonnet was a fashionable headdress during the first half of the nineteenth century. Hats began to replace bonnets before the Civil War period. By 1880 hats became symbolic of the emancipation of women in America. (9:147) The adoption of a hat meant the acceptance of worldly fashion and signified a change in social status for a woman.

Bonnets were worn by the sisters in the church throughout the nineteenth century and by a majority of the sisters during the first quarter of the twentieth century. They were considered a "plain" item of dress in contrast to fashionable

hats. A bonnet was worn over a prayer cap. These two items should not be confused; they were separate items and not interchangeable. The bonnet did not have the religious significance of the cap. No specific scripture could be cited which required a sister to wear one. Socially, it identified the wearer as a member of a religious sect and therefore as holding certain beliefs. A woman who wished to join the church not only had to make confession of faith, but also to accept the status implied by the bonnet and to deny herself the wearing of fashionable hats.

The type of headdress that the sisters could wear was an issue before the Annual Meeting of 1849. "Can it be allowed for... sister to wear trimmed straw and leghorn bonnets." (90:132) The answer given to Article 3 was negative. Although no specific scripture could be pointed out, the wearing of a hat as a head covering was considered inconsistent with the Word of God. It signified conformity to the fashions of the world, as denounced in Romans 12:2. The decision of 1849 was upheld in 1866, Article 27. (90:313) Members who failed to comply after being admonished more than once were to be dealt with according to Matthew 18.

The issue was again clearly stated in 1876, Article 21.

> Is it wrong for sisters to wear fashionable hats instead of bonnets? And where is the Scripture forbidding the wearing of such hats?
> Answer: We decide it is wrong according to Rom. 12:2; I Tim. 2:9. (90:419)

As a means of disciplining the offender, the sacrament of the bread was to be withheld from a sister, who wore a hat to the communion table, Article 16, 1877. (91:349) The customary procedure for the distribution of the bread among the sisters was for a ministering elder to pass along the table and give a piece to each sister at the table. A quick glance told him the difference between a cap and bonnet or a hat. A communicant wearing a hat had pride and therefore could not be served because she would be guilty of eating the bread unworthily. Elders who permitted sisters to wear hats at the communion table, or any other time for that matter, were to be considered as transgressors and dealt with accordingly.

A sister who wore a hat was subject to being excommunicated from the church by the action of the local church council and having her name struck from the roll. Inconsistencies in handling cases of discipline were an issue brought before the Annual Meeting of 1897, Article 3. (91:654) The names of men who wore many of the styles and fashions of the world were retained on the roll. The restricting of membership only to sisters who wore bonnets and caps was perceived as an inconsistency between the two sexes. A committee was appointed to study the issue, but no sisters were appointed to the committee. The reason was that committees were chosen from Standing Committee, which consisted of only ordained elders. Sisters who had become exhorters were not advanced to the eldership. A woman's influence was private as she discussed issues with her husband. The report brought by the above committee before the Annual Meeting of 1898 under Article 3 asked for no further decisions, but adherence to those which had been made already. (91:669)

Sisters who desired to dismiss the fashions of the world found the wearing of plain bonnets to be consistent with the style of their plain dresses and appropriate to wear over their caps. They believed that they were abiding by the scriptures by not conforming to worldly fashions. The bonnet and cap were a silent testimony to their beliefs. Ordinarily a sister removed her bonnet during a church service and laid it beside her on the bench. If the bench were crowded, the ties were again tied and slipped over her wrist. Presiding elders often chastised sisters for not removing their bonnets during services.

Bonnets were made for both summer and winter wear with the fabric selected for the season. They differed in size, shape, and method of stiffening the brim. The winter bonnet shown in Figure 91 was handmade of brown worsted and featured the deep brim and long shoulder cape. Since this fabric did not permit starching, the brim was stiffened by inserting one and one-fourth inch strips of cardboard into slots produced by hand stitching. A bonnet stiffened in this manner was called a "slat bonnet". The front edge of this bonnet was finished by a double fold of fabric turned back over the brim. The edge of the crown was turned under and hand sewn to the outside of the brim. Two ties were attached inside the brim for tying under the chin. Two other ties were attached to the corner of the brim on the outside of the bonnet. When tied, they covered the juncture of the crown and shoulder cape. Bonnets of this type were worn before 1890. The slat bonnet shown in Figure 92 had a flared brim, but retained the square shoulder cape. Black silk taffeta was used for this bonnet which did not permit starching.

Brims of bonnets were stiffened also with crinoline, buckram, and even cardboard. The rows of quilting used to hold the layers of fabric in place followed the edge of the brim. Cotton wadding was placed over the stiffening before hand quilting the brim of the bonnet shown in Figure 93. Rows of machine stitching were used to stiffen the bonnet shown in Figure 94. The edge of the brim extended well into the crown of this bonnet. This permitted the pleating of the edge of the crown to remain in a stable position, adding a decorative touch. Due to aging, the black silk taffeta fabric of the crown broke at this point, despite the support given by a lining. Satin ribbon was used for the ties.

Bonnets worn at the end of the nineteenth century were modified in three ways: the shoulder cape was shortened, the brim was reduced in width, and decorative touches were added giving individuality. The bonnet shown in Figure 95 permitted more of the face to show when

76

Figure 91. Worsted Slat Bonnet With Square Cape.

Figure 92. Silk Slat Bonnet With Flared Brim.

Figure 93. Quilted Bonnet With Square Cape.

Figure 94. Quilted Bonnet With Rounded Cape.

observed from the side. The shoulder cape, now called a "frill", barely touched the shoulders, The crown was attached to the brim with decorative cartridge pleats. A summer bonnet of black organdy is shown in Figure 96. The brim was cut even more narrow and the shoulder cape was reduced to a one-inch frill at the neckline. A decorative touch was achieved by triple rows of stitching on the brim and by adding a ruffle to all edges of the brim.

Two rather unusual bonnets are shown in Figures 97 and 98. The corner of the brim of the first one extended well below the chin line of the face, and reached the corner of the frill. The brim was stiffened with one-inch strips of cardboard placed lengthwise of the brim. Sheet wadding, placed over the cardboard, gave a padded effect between the rows of hand stitching. The outer fabric was blue and gold changeable silk taffeta. The lining was blue cambric and the inside of the brim was overlaid with sheer white China silk. A narrow piping at the edge of the brim and between the crown and brim gave an elegant touch. The brim of the second bonnet was made of wine colored straw which matched in color the silk taffeta crown and frill.

The exquisite bonnet shown in Figure 99 is a silent witness to the skill of its maker. The fullness at the edge of the crown was applied to the brim with fine cartridge pleats. In all probability the edge was stiffened in some manner before pleating. The black silk taffeta was stretched over the slightly flared brim. The edge of the brim was finished with a piping of white silk. The tucked bias decorative detail on the brim was used also on the frill. The winter bonnet shown in Figure 100 was made of dark maroon velveteen. A folded strip of the fabric was used to cover the seam which joined the crown to the brim. Ribbon was used to cover the seam at the neckline and for the ties.

By 1895 even Brethren bonnets came in many sizes, shapes, and colors. The editor of *The Gos-pel Messenger* had something to say regarding the color of the bonnets of the sisters.

> Our sisters often destroy wonderfully the beauty of their dressing in the choosing of colors... at one of our late Annual Meetings... it was a noticeable feature in the apparel of our sisters... sisters who were dressed in pure, clean white, which is plain and modest, and all right, but on their heads they wore red bonnets,–as red as scarlet. Others wore black dresses and pink bonnets, and still others, brown dresses with green bonnets. Indeed, we cannot think of any shade in color that was not represented in bonnets, at that meeting. While this may not have been considered a violation of order, in dressing, yet it certainly was and is a violation of harmony in color in dressing for beauty. It should be remembered that there is as much immodesty in the arranging and choosing of color in apparel, as there is in the form and cut... The Christian world has accepted white, black, gray and drab as being plain and modest colors for dressing. And these, not all at one time, but such use of them as seems to harmonize with good taste and the true standard of the beautiful. Anything that detracts from the comeliness of the human form, in dressing, robs us of our native beauty and is a violation of the true idea of dressing or apparel. (120:201)

Seeking greater uniformity within the church, members of the Oakland Church requested the Annual Meeting of 1900 "to adopt one style of bonnet for our sisters, with less expense and in keeping with our profession, instead of the five styles, with superfluity of naughtiness." (68:76) The answer formulated by Standing Committee to return the query from whence it came was adopted by the delegate body. The reason for the return of the query was explained by a member of the Standing Committee.

> The reason we agreed to return this paper is because we have old sisters, and we have a custom that was used some years ago, and to make a change would not be fair; all that is necessary is to require that they shall be plain, and we thought it was

Figure 95. Bonnet With Moderate Size Brim and Frill.

Figure 96. Quilted Summer Bonnet Without Frill.

Figure 97. Handmade Bonnet of Silk Taffeta.

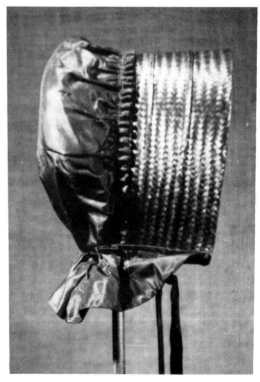

Figure 98. Silk Bonnet With Straw Brim.

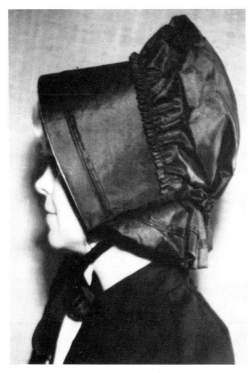

Figure 99. Exquisite Bonnet With Flared Brim.

Figure 100. Winter Bonnet of Red Velveteen.

Figure 101. Three Sisters Wearing Wire-Framed Bonnets, 1906.

requiring too much of our sisters, and consequently we decided to return it. (68:77)

Members took positions on both sides of the issue requiring sisters to wear bonnets. Some feared the loss of bonnets would weaken the church because of conforming to the fashions of the world. Others felt that the affirmation of faith did not include a bonnet. To an evangelistic church, the holding of lost souls at abeyance because of not adopting the bonnet brought a dilemma. However, the former position of Annual Meeting was upheld by the dress decision of 1911, as stated in Article 3, Section 3, "That plain bonnets and hoods be the head-dress." (80:5) The report of a committee on "Differences of Practice and Teaching" was adopted by Annual meeting of 1920. "Sisters wearing hats" were referred to the dress decision of 1911. (86:11) Since that time there has been no formal statement before Annual Meeting concerning the wearing of bonnets or hats. The decision of 1911 remained in effect in 1970.

Attempts were made to enforce the decision in various ways. Elders admonished the sisters in their congregations for not wearing a bonnet. Mothers chided their daughters for not wearing one. Sunday school superintendents spoke to teachers who did not set an example for their pupils. (206) Small children were permitted and sometimes prompted to wear one before joining the church. Hopefully they would desire to wear a bonnet rather than a hat later in life.

An article in favor of bonnets appeared in *The Gospel Messenger* in 1912. The author wrote that she wore a bonnet because she loved "gospel plainness", it was appropriate with a plain dress, it was convenient, it gave good protection from the elements, it was inexpensive to make, it served as an equalizer between the rich and poor, it was not affected by the changes of fashion, it was a witness against pride and lust, and it meant something to the sisters within the church. (165:710) Perhaps the greatest point in favor of a bonnet was that it did not look like a hat

in anybody's imagination. Thus a sister who wore a bonnet was set apart from women of the world who wore hats.

Further modification of the bonnet took place after 1900. The width of the brim was narrowed until it no longer protruded beyond the face. The shoulder cape or frill was left off. Both the crown and the brim were reduced in size and stiffened with wire frames. Three young sisters wearing bonnets of this type are shown in Figure 101. The chenille yarns in a zig-zag pattern gave a pleasing texture to the wide straw braid used to cover the wire frame of the bonnet shown in Figure 102. Fabrics used for covering the frames were chiffon, coarse net, straw braid, and velvet in black, brown, and buff. Narrow braid, self fabric, and satin ribbon were used for trimming.

Later in the twentieth century pressed felt forms were used to stiffen both the bonnet crown and brim. They were trimmed to fit the shape of the head and the amount and manner of wearing the hair. The fabric was drawn over the pressed felt forms and fastened with hand stitching. Some decorative technique was used to cover the juncture of the crown and brim such as a flattened bias tube made from the bonnet fabric. The frill consisted merely of a bias edging used to finish the neckline. The bonnet shown in Figure 103 was fastened at the side of the chin. Two short pieces of ribbon, one longer than the other, were joined by means of a hook and eye. The corner of the bonnet shown in Figure 104 was reduced in size, making this headdress barely visible when viewed from the front.

Like the cap, the discarding of the brim of the bonnet left only the crown. A bonnet of this type fits very closely to the back of the head. If the crown is stiffened with a wire frame, it is called a bonnet. If no frame is used, it is called a "turban". One turban examined by the author was soft enough to roll in the hand without damaging it. The edge was finished with

Figure 102. Wire-Framed Bonnet, Alice Wagner.

Figure 103. Bonnet Stiffened With Pressed Felt Forms.

Figure 104. Small Bonnet, Nellie Hollinger, 1968.

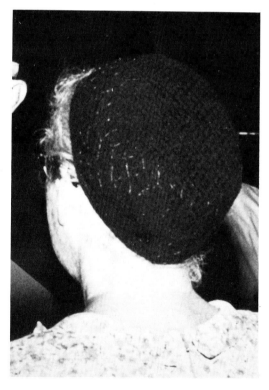

Figure 105. Turban, Back View, 1969.

a reverse tucked strip of bias fabric applied very skillfully. The appearance is the same for both the bonnet and turban, when placed on the head. Figure 105 shows either a bonnet or turban worn by an unidentified sister attending the Annual Meeting of 1969, held at Louisville, Kentucky. A small one- or two-piece cap is worn under a bonnet of this type. Bonnets of this type were adopted after 1940.

Ordinarily sisters made their own bonnets. Mary Teeter wrote in 1912 that the fabric for a bonnet cost $1.10 and would last from two to five years. (165:710) Sisters who did not make their own bonnets found that it was expensive to hire them made, costing as much as $7.00 in 1910. One sister was chided for having laid aside her bonnet for a hat. She retorted that her hat cost $2.00 and a bonnet cost $10.00. (206)

A method for taking measurements for a bonnet appeared in an advertisement in a church publication in 1906. (104) Three measurements were needed: length over the head, width across the back of the neck, and the width of the brim. (Figure 106) Sisters in eastern Pennsylvania who made their own bonnets were able to purchase all the necessary materials at plain clothing stores or departments in other stores catering to plainly dressed customers. The wire frames used to make the two-piece bonnets shown in Figure 107 were available at Hager's Store in Lancaster, Pennsylvania, in 1968. These frames can be adjusted to fit the size of the head, the amount of hair, and the manner in which the long hair was worn. The fabric was drawn over the frame and fastened by hand sewing. The lining for the brim was usually shirred in some manner. Modest but pleasing decorative touches were added. Sometimes one end of the neck ribbon was fashioned into a rosette and secured with a few stitches. The end of the other piece of ribbon was hemmed. A relatively large hook and eye were applied to the ends of the ribbon. When wearing the bonnet, the hook and eye were hidden behind the rosette which rested at the side of the chin.

The pressed felt forms needed for making the two-piece bonnet shown in Figure 103 were also available at Hagar's Store in 1968. (213) The crowns came in two shapes and cost $1.25 each. One brim piece was used for all styles, costing $0.50. (Figure 108) Both the crown and brim pieces were trimmed by the seamstress to fit the head of the sister and the shape of the bonnet desired. The fabric was drawn over the outside of the crown and pleated at the edge to make it conform to the shape of the crown. It was then secured by hand stitching. The brim was covered with fabric also. Usually the lining was given a decorative touch in some way. Bonnet fabrics offered for sale in 1968 were matelassé, coarse lace, and embossed knits in black and navy for less than $3.00 per yard. (Figure 109) Three-fourths yard of forty-five inch fabric was considered adequate for one bonnet.

A bonnet pin was used with a bonnet made without ties. (Figure 110) This was a new item for the sister in the church, but one which had been used with fashionable hats for many years. Thus it was readily available in millinery stores.

Patterns for making bonnets shown in Figures 102 through 105 were not available since the pieces of fabric were drawn over the frames and the excess trimmed away during the construction process. Written directions for making a bonnet have not been located by the author. The sisters who made bonnets on consignment at the Marian and Ruth Shop in Mount Joy, Pennsylvania, hesitated to take time from their work to answer questions and explain procedures. Another sister was willing to explain the procedure, but a demonstration was impossible without buying supplies. This she hesitated to do because she no longer wore a bonnet.

Although the demise of the bonnet has been extensive across the sisterhood, it has not been completed. A few older sisters, particularly in the eastern part of the United States, continue to wear bonnets. The majority of the sisters

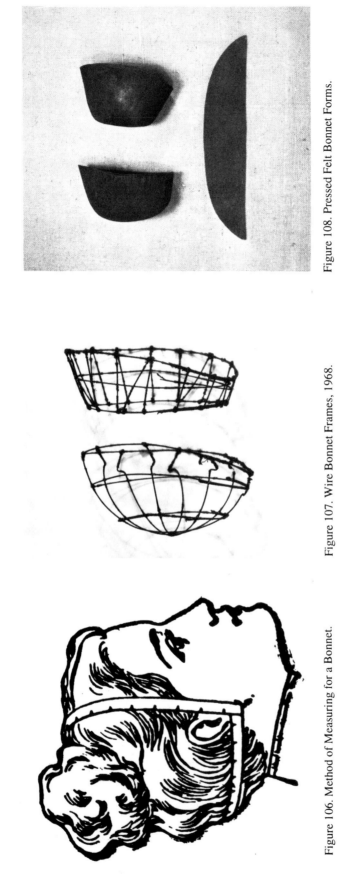

Figure 108. Pressed Felt Bonnet Forms.

Figure 107. Wire Bonnet Frames, 1968.

Figure 106. Method of Measuring for a Bonnet.

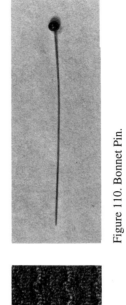

Figure 110. Bonnet Pin.

Figure 109. Bonnet Fabrics, 1968.

observed wearing a bonnet in 1968 through 1970 wore either the small two-piece bonnets shown in Figures 103 and 104, or the smaller one-piece bonnet or turban shown in Figure 105. The question arose whether society at large identifies the wearer of a bonnet as holding particular religious beliefs, or labels her as "peculiar".

Sunbonnets were worn to church by the sisters on hot summer days. Figure 111 shows a summer bonnet worn before 1875. It had a deep brim, extending well beyond the face, and a cape extending over the shoulders. The brim was partially stiffened by rows of machine stitching through a double layer of fabric. Additional stiffening was achieved by starching, since it was made of a washable cotton fabric. The fabric featured alternate rows of plain and twill weave. A cord, inserted into a casing across the back at the neckline, permitted adjustment in the size of the crown and facilitated ironing it. The back ties were cut on the bias and hemmed neatly. The ties used under the chin were cut straight of the fabric and hemmed also. The decorative detail was not rickrack, but small pieces of the fabric folded into points and inserted in the seam at the edge of the brim.

A slat bonnet of pink-checked cotton gingham is shown in Figure 112. The strip of fabric turned back over the brim was edged with lace. The cardboard strips were removed during washing and ironing. This style bonnet was worn before 1890.

An unusual sunbonnet is shown in Figure 113. The crown and rounded shoulder cape were attached to the brim by means of buttons and buttonholes. This permitted heavy starching of the slightly-flared, diagonally-quilted brim. The scalloped edges of the brim and shoulder cape were bound with the same brown-checked printed fabric used for the bonnet.

The brim of the sunbonnet shown in Figure 114 was stiffened with flat pieces of cornstalks. The strips were cut from between two nodes of a dry stalk. After dressing and shaping, the strips were inserted into slots stitched in the brim of the bonnet. The strips of cornstalk were found to be very durable, and the bonnet could be washed without removing them. No starching was required for a bonnet of this type. Between 1920 and 1930 sisters at the Pine Creek Church in northern Indiana made cornstalk sunbonnets to sell.

The modifications in size and shape observed in the other bonnets discussed were not found in sunbonnets. With the increased use of the automobile in summer, they were no longer worn to church. Many sisters discarded them even for daily wear. Only a very few sisters wore them for outdoor work as late as 1960.

Dresses. The one- or two-piece dress worn by the sisters during the first half of the nineteenth century had a fitted bodice, long fitted sleeves, and long full skirt. There was little difference in cut of a dress worn on Sunday and that worn daily, or that worn in winter or summer. An illustration in Nead's *Theological Writings*, published in 1850, shows this style of dress. (Figure 115) It should be noted that the dresses in this illustration were not covered with either a cape or an apron.

Hoops for extending the full skirts of dresses became fashionable during the Civil War. The Brethren frowned upon sisters who wore hoops. Article 3 of the minutes of the Annual Meeting of 1861 stated that the church had a right to deal with said offenders. (90:249) They were to be considered as disobedient members if they did not lay their hoops aside. This position was reaffirmed by the Annual Meeting of 1862 and 1863. Elizabeth Tulley became a member of the Philadelphia Church at age fifteen. Her wedding picture, taken in 1868, shows that she wore hoops for the occasion. (Figure 116)

The skirts of fashionable dresses worn in the 1880's were aptly described in Article 12 of the minutes of the Annual Meeting for 1886.

Inasmuch as necessity required a

85

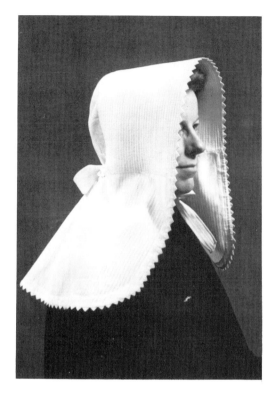

Figure 111. Summer Bonnet of Sarah Melling Rupel, 1875.

Figure 112. Slat Bonnet of Pink Checked Gingham.

Figure 113. Quilted Bonnet With Button-On Crown and Frill.

Figure 114. Cornstalk Slat Sunbonnet.

Figure 115. Dress With Fitted Bodice and Sleeve, c. 1850.

Figure 116. Dress With Hoops, Elizabeth Miller, 1868.

Figure 117. A Sister's Plain Dress Contrasted With Fashionable Dress, c. 1880.

specification in the order of dress to be worn by the brethren, we therefore petition Annual Meeting through District Meeting to make the time honored custom of wearing the plain cap or kerchief in connection with a plain skirt dress a specification for the order or uniform to be worn by the sisters, as many of them are departing from the gospel plainness as interpreted by our fathers and church, thus destroying that oneness and admitting in its stead the popular fashions of a proud world.

Answer: We decide that gospel plainness required our sisters to attire themselves in plainly made garments, free from ornaments, ruffles, and all unnecessary appendages, and that it is the duty of all housekeepers to see that our sisters are properly instructed concerning the necessity of this gospel plainness, and it is also their duty to see that the order of the church, respecting plainness, is properly carried out in their respective congregations, both upon the part of the brethren as well as the sisters. (91:452)

The contrast between the fashion of the world of this period and the plainness of dress of an older sister in the church in shown in Figure 117. The mother was a member of the church, but not her two daughters. The mother was wearing also the dress cape, apron, and cap; whereas her daughters were not.

With the demise of the apron and dress cape, the silhouette of the dress and of its wearer became evident. As new silhouettes came into vogue young sisters adopted them, while older sisters retained what they had adopted when they were young. It was possible to date plain dresses worn after 1880 because they reflected some elements of fashionable dress. The Basque wedding dress shown in Figure 118 was worn in 1885. The separate skirt reached the floor. The high neckline was featured in fashionable dresses at that time. The close spacing of the buttons and buttonholes was necessary because the bodice was fitted so tightly. The white edging at the neck and sleeve gave a pleasing accent to this dark colored dress. Also it protected the

dress from soil and could be removed for laundering. Dresses with a pointed bodice were fashionable in the early 1890's. This point was featured also in the sister's dress shown in Figure 119. Two other features of fashionable dresses appeared in the dresses of the sisters: fullness at the top of the sleeve and gores in the skirt. A sister wearing a "plain" dress with these two features is shown in Figure 120.

The wedding dresses selected by the sisters followed fashionable dresses in regard to cut and fabric selected. The light-colored wedding dress, shown in Figure 121, was worn about 1896 and was in contrast to the darker ones of the previous decade. Closer examination of a winter dress in this same style revealed other design and construction details. (Figures 122A and 122B) Fabric covered buttons were closely spaced at the front opening. The gored skirt was arranged in pleats at the waistline to give added fullness in the back. The fabric was a high-quality black wool. Velvet was used to edge the neckline and cuffs. The dress was lined throughout with cambric. Extra stiffening, from six to ten inches wide, was used at the hem. The hem fold was protected from wear by the application of a heavy wool braid placed on the underside.

The tight fit of the bodice of the dress shown in Figures 123A and 123B was achieved by both seaming and darting. Skirts were not always gathered in their entirety at the waistline as this one was done. Sometimes the gathers were deleted across the center front. The neckline of this dress was finished with a band of fabric of sufficient width to turn down. Some sisters continued to wear this style of dress as late as 1950.

Dresses worn by the sisters at the end of the first decade of the twentieth century featured vertical tucks in the bodice and separate gored skirts. (Figure 124A and 124B) The sleeve of this dress was gathered to a band at the wrist and also into the armscye at the cap. The

Figure 118. Basque Dress, Anna Miller Royer, 1885.

Figure 119. Pointed Waistline on Dress, Anna Hildreth.

Figure 120. Plain Dress With Fashionable Silhouette.

Figure 121. Wedding Dress, Mabel Bashor Weaver, c. 1896.

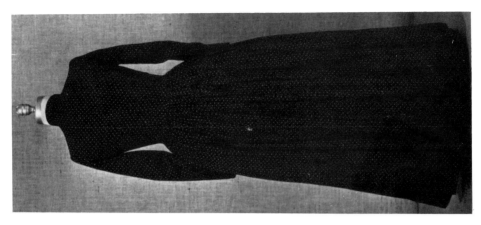

Figure 123B. Back View.

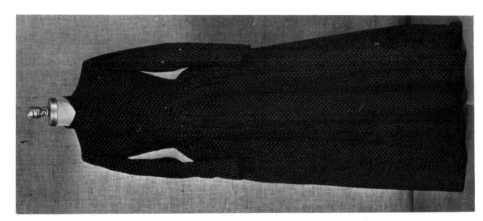

Figure 123A. "Plain" Dress of Black Cotton.

Figure 122B. Back View.

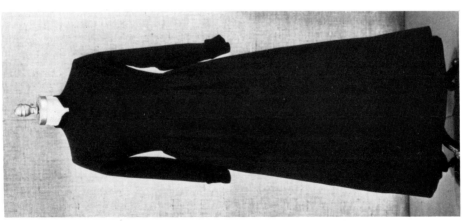

Figure 122A. Worsted Dress With Velvet Trimming.

90

Figure 124A. Winter Dress in "Simple" Style, 1914.

Figure 124B. Back View.

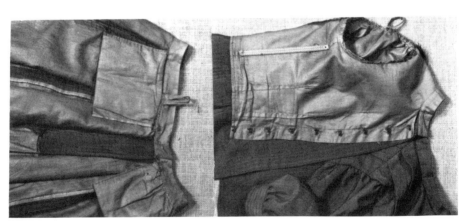

Figure 124C. Construction Detail.

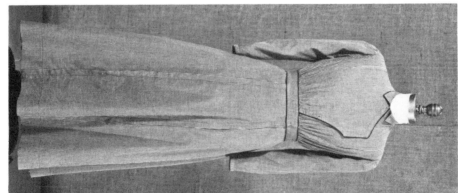

Figure 125. Gingham Dress for Summer.

neckband was not attached to the neckline of the dress, but was made as a separate piece. A similar band or belt was used as a decorative finish at the waist. Three gores were used for the front of the skirt. Back emphasis was achieved by fullness from pleating two extra wide gores. The dress was ankle length.

Construction details found on the inside of the dress are shown in Figure 124C. Cambric was used to line both the bodice and the skirt. The bodice shaping was maintained by stays attached to the vertical seams and darts. Hooks and eyes were used for the front bodice closures on both the lining and the outer fabric. Hip pads were inserted to achieve the fashionable silhouette or to compensate for physical inadequacies. Loops fastened to each armscye seam and inside the skirt band provided a means for hanging up each piece of the garment. A garment was turned wrong side out and the loops were slipped onto hooks spaced twelve to fourteen inches apart on wooden strips on the bedroom wall. This dress was handmade from a fabric of wool and cotton, called "brilliantine". Moths have damaged the fabric, removing only the wool from the filling yarns.

The dress shown in Figure 125 was made of black and white one-eighth inch checked gingham. The Gibson Girl style has been modified in that the seven-gore skirt fitted the waistband without gathers or pleats. The vertical tucks at the shoulders did not extend to the waistband. Instead the fullness was gathered to the waistband. The collar, sleeve, waistband, and asymmetric front closure of the dress were piped in black. The edge of the hem was machine-stitched, the custom of the day. In summer this dress was worn to church and other social occasions in the local community.

By 1900 more sisters received an education than previously. Graduation exercises from the eighth grade and high school brought new demands on the wardrobe. Special dresses were made for these occasions and later were worn to church. The fashionable silhouette shown in Figure 126 featured only a few of the decorative details customary of dresses of the day. Often these dresses were of a two-piece style with the juncture at the waistline covered in some manner. A ribbon with a large bow was used in this instance. Accessories for this graduation occasion included white shoes, mits, and a watch tucked under the waistband of the skirt.

The wearing of blouses, or "waists" as they were called, and skirts became popular with the sisters during the first decade of the twentieth century. When white waists were worn with white skirts, the effect was that of a white dress. This effect was new in a sister's wardrobe. When a white waist was worn with a black skirt, this value contrast was new also. (Figure 127) A velvet ribbon at the waistline gave a pleasing contrast in texture.

Suits were accepted by women who entered the business world. Some blouses blended with the color of the skirt or suit. (Figure 128) This bride of 1910 wore a jeweled buckle on her belt. She removed her suit jacket for her wedding picture. Perhaps when the jacket was put on, it gave the appearance of the suit worn by an unidentified sister attending the Annual Meeting at Winona Lake, Indiana, in 1913. (Figure 129) This was the only photograph located by the author which showed a sister wearing a suit. Suits were accepted but the extent they were worn has not been determined.

The dress decision of 1911 stated under Article 3, Section 2, "That the sisters attire themselves in plainly-made garments, free from ornaments and unnecessary appendages." (80:5) One contributor to *The Gospel Messenger* in 1911 listed the trimmings inappropriate for a plain dress as "lace, fringe, embroidery, braid, and strips of velvet." (155:379) A second contributor warned against pride as evidenced in "skirts with many unnecessary gores, embroideries, lace, collars, shiny and showy dress goods, tightly laced corsets, unnecessary tucks." (156:35)

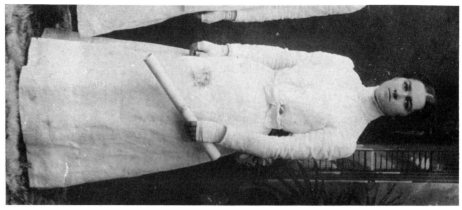

Figure 126. Graduation Dress, Susie Merchant, c. 1900.

Figure 127. Skirt and Waist, Effie B. Rupel, c. 1902.

Figure 128. Skirt and Waist, Florence Replogle, 1910.

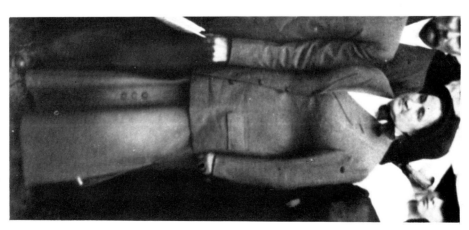

Figure 129. Suit Worn to Annual Meeting, 1913.

Sisters varied in the amount of decorative detail each permitted on a garment. The black silk blouse with high neck and long sleeves shown in Figure 130A was worn about 1910. It could not be criticized as to color or cut. However, the elegant touch of soutache braid, shown in detail in Figure 130B, would have been considered out of place by a sister who dressed more plainly. White was considered a "modest" color for a waist worn in the second decade of the twentieth century. The white waist shown in Figure 131A and 131B also featured a high neck treatment and long sleeves. Sheer fabrics brought criticism because they exposed the arms and chest and undergarments. (156:35) Decorative undergarments were criticized because of the time and money required to produce them.

In 1910 a white two-piece dress was chosen by the bride for her wedding at Spokane, Washington. (Figure 132) Features of the dress–the high neck, tucked yoke, and long skirt–were in contrast to the dress of the bride in the next illustration. Figure 133 shows a bride of 1920 wearing her handmade dress featuring a collar and decorative crosswise tucks in a shorter skirt.

The two-piece dresses shown in Figures 134 and 135 are representative of the cotton dresses worn in summer by older sisters after 1920. The style was in sharp contrast to the fashionable dresses of that decade. These dresses were handmade from modest printed fabrics available in local dry goods stores. When doing physical labor, these sisters protected their dresses with aprons, but laid them aside when attending church.

The predominate style of plain dress worn by some sisters in Pennsylvania in 1968 is shown in Figures 136A and 136B. The bodice was fitted by means of tucks at the shoulders and gathers at the waist. The front opening was fastened by hooks and eyes. The neckline was finished with fitted facing. The sleeves were cut in one piece. The skirt was constructed of six gores and reached slightly below the calf of the leg.

The fabric was a sheer worsted wool, charcoal gray in color, with a slight tweed effect. This dress was not worn without its matching cape with attached band. This dress was handmade, showing considerable skill. Patterns for plain dresses were handmade also. (182)

For those sisters who chose to buy their plain dresses, this same style was available in 1968 at Hager's Store in Lancaster, Pennsylvania, and at the Marian and Ruth Shop in Mount Joy, Pennsylvania. Fabrics selected for her plain dresses by one sister are shown in Figure 137. The swatches she sent the author were grey worsted, black cotton madras, black and white cotton printed voile and batiste, black and navy cotton shagbark, and black and white pinchecks in nylon and Dacron. She explained that small-patterned fabrics were difficult to find unless a store catered to the needs of sisters who dressed plainly. (184)

Neckerchiefs and Dress Capes. Neckerchiefs and small capes were a prominent part of the dress of the sisters in the nineteenth century. The author is of the opinion that they were a continuation of the fichu worn in the eighteenth century.

A small square of fabric, or kerchief, was worn often about the neck and therefore was called a "neckerchief". A white neckerchief was worn by the sister shown in Figure 138. Other sisters wore black ones. The neckerchief was worn in addition to the dress cape, if the latter was worn. It protected the neckline of the dress or cape from soil and added a contrasting touch of color or texture. From the photographs observed, the assumption has been made that neckerchiefs were laid aside by the end of the nineteenth century.

Dress capes were also a distinctive part of the dress of the sisters in the nineteenth century. However, illustrations in Nead's *Theological Writings* published in 1850, do not show the sisters wearing dress capes. (Figure 115) Capes varied in color: white, black, matching, or in

Figure 130A. Black Silk Taffeta Waist.

Figure 130B. Detail of Soutache Braid.

Figure 131A. White Sheer Cotton Waist.

Figure 131B. Back View.

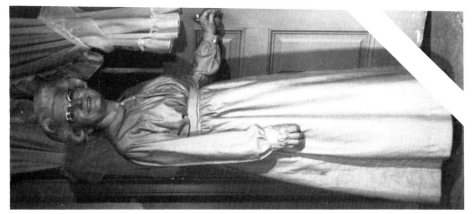

Figure 135. Cotton Dress of Laura Madeira, c. 1926.

Figure 134. Cotton Dress, Ann Hummel Blough (1842-1921).

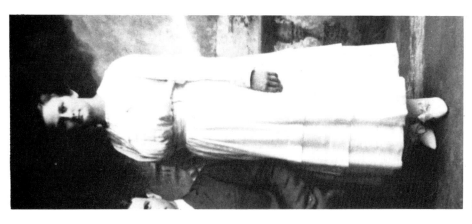

Figure 133. Wedding Dress, Mary Hay Rinehart, 1920.

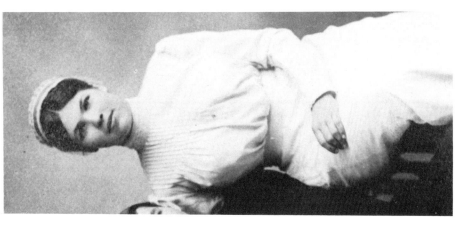

Figure 132. Wedding Dress, Elsie Aschenbrenner, 1910.

Figure 136A. "Plain" Dress of Mary Lutz Snyder (1866-1948).

Figure 136B. Back View.

Figure 137. Swatches of Fabrics Selected for "Plain" Dresses, 1969.

Figure 138. White Neckerchief With Dress Cape.

Figure 139. Square Cape, Sarah Rupel, c. 1875.

Figure 140. Dress Cape, Elizabeth Wise Royer (1843-1924).

Figure 141. Square Dress Cape, Sarah Lewis.

contrast to the dress. They varied in shape: square, circular, or triangular. The purpose of wearing a cape seemed a bit elusive. At least four sisters told the author that a large dress cape served as a modesty piece. Not only did it hide the physical form of a woman, but a baby could be nursed less conspicuously.

At least some of the dress capes worn at mid-century or slightly later were white. A white square cape with heavier yarns inserted to form a border was worn by the sister shown in Figure 139. This picture was taken before her death in 1875. The white cape is in contrast to her patterned apron and dark dress. Black square capes, folded diagonally, were also worn at this time and as late as the first quarter of the twentieth century. (Figure 140) A decorative edging of a contrasting texture was added to the cape shown in Figure 141.

Dress capes cut in a circular manner eliminated the fold formed at the neckline by a square cape. By cutting a portion of the fabric away at the neck edge, the fabric laid smoothly about the neck. The printed cape shown in Figure 142 appears to have been made in this manner. The fabric used for the cape in Figure 143 matched the dress fabric chosen by this bride for her wedding in 1857. Circular capes were convenient when the outer garment was a shawl.

The addition of a seam at the shoulder permitted a more economical use of fabric than was possible with a circular cape. Further curving of the shoulder seam gave even a better fit over the shoulder area than was achieved without it. But this seaming did not allow the cape to lie flat for ironing. These capes were made of a single thickness of fabric. This not only reduced the amount of fabric required, but also made them lighter in weight for hot summer days. The neckline was finished with either a fitted facing, a narrow band, a wider band turned down, or a small collar. The lower edge was sometimes hemmed, faced, or finished with a decorative braid. (Figure 144) A cape of similar

width at the shoulder is also shown in Figure 145. It was worn by this bride of fifty years for her golden wedding celebration in 1954.

As coats became more popular the lower edge of the dress cape was trimmed off to permit a sister's arm to enter the sleeve of the coat without wrinkling the cape. This modification decreased the width of the cape at the shoulders until it barely covered the armscye seam of the dress. Thus the line produced by the lower edge of the cape was gradually changed from an arc to a V in back and a double V in front. This triangular shaped cape was sometimes called a "three-cornered" cape. The triangular cape shown in Figure 146 was made of barred black cotton. The neckband was turned down giving the effect of a small collar. The sister shown in Figure 147 wore this style cape in a Pennsylvania schoolroom in 1912.

Capes received less wear than dresses and therefore certain ones have remained as relics. Sisters who laid aside the cape continued to wear plain dresses. Some sisters laid aside their capes slightly before 1900, whereas others retained a cape of some type until 1970. Apparently the cape was laid aside before the apron in midwestern United States, but the opposite was true in the eastern part of the country.

Another style of dress cape, not worn in the nineteenth century, was adopted by the sisters in the eastern part of the Brotherhood. No evidence has been located that this style of cape was worn in Indiana or farther west. This style of cape is shown in Figure 148 and was worn with the dress shown in Figure 136. The cape was attached to a waistband in both front and back. The waistband was opened on the left side. A neck placket was located at center front. The neck edge was protected by a narrow white piping which could be removed for laundering. The width of the front and back bodice portions extended to the armscye. One or two small pleats or dart tucks were inserted at the lower edge of the cape before it was attached to the

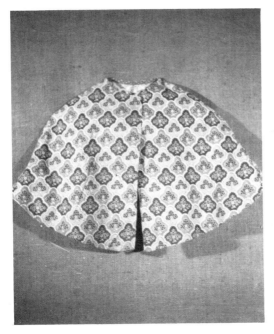

Figure 142. Round Dress Cape With Shoulder Seam.

Figure 143. Dress Cape, Mary Smith Senger, 1857.

Figure 144. Dress Cape, Mary Magdalena Cripe, c. 1911.

Figure 145. Dress Cape, Barbara Longenecker, 1954.

Figure 146. Triangular Dress Cape With Neckband.

Figure 148. Dress Cape With Waistband.

Figure 147. Triangular Cape, Minnie Ginker, 1912.

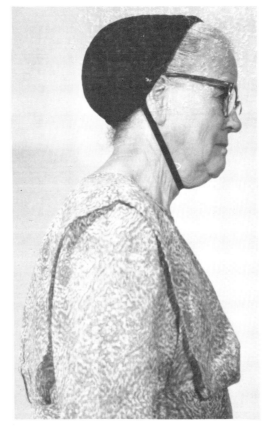

Figure 149. Dress Cape, Nellie Hollinger, 1968.

waistband. This reduction in the width of the lower edge improved the fit of the cape over the bust and shoulder blade areas. The side appearance of a cape of this style is shown in Figure 149. It matched the summer dress made of gray and white voile.

An assumption was made by the author and confirmed by Anna Bashore Keeney of Bethel, Pennsylvania, that this last style of dress cape with waistband originated from the triangular cape. Often the corners of the latter were pinned to the waistband of the apron to prevent them from becoming soiled while kneading bread and doing other work. (190) In time the waistband was sewn to the cape and the apron discarded. Thus the cape was retained as a modesty piece. The apron, symbolic of work, was discarded from the Sunday dress.

Aprons. Aprons continued to be an important part of the dress of the sisters in the nineteenth century and were worn early in the twentieth century. All aprons were "half aprons"; that is they consisted only of a skirt portion attached to a band. The band was pinned about the waist or was of sufficient length to tie. The hem of the apron fell either even with the lower edge of the long dress, or slightly above it; or at the knee, or slightly above it. The fabric varied according to the season and occasion. White or black aprons were customary for Sunday wear. Calico or gingham aprons were worn during the week.

The black knee-length apron shown in Figure 150 was without fullness across the front at the waistline. This lack of fullness was also found in dress skirts after 1870. Having one's picture taken was a dress-up occasion. It has been assumed that the white apron in Figure 151 was also worn to church on Sunday. The two sisters shown in Figure 152 wore aprons with a slight flare, produced by gores. Sometime after 1885 the apron fabric matched the dress and cape, giving a unified appearance to the ensemble as shown in this illustration.

Of the aprons located, four were selected as representative of those worn during this period. A nut brown worsted apron is shown in Figure 153. The ties were a continuation of the band, 84 inches long in all. The body of the apron was 32 inches long and 58 inches wide at the hem. The width of the apron was wider than one piece of fabric. Fabrics were manufactured in narrow widths at this time. More width was achieved by splitting a second length of fabric and adding this half panel to each side of the first. Seaming the center front of a garment would have "spoiled" the appearance in the eyes of the seamstress of that time. Gathers were used to control the fullness at the waistline of the black sateen apron shown in Figure 154.

A white apron of plain cotton fabric with seven rows of tucking and a lace edging is shown in Figure 155. Sometimes a washable white apron featured a large pocket. Often it contained a neatly folded handkerchief and money for the offering. Children hoped that there were peppermint lozenges ere the service became too long. (191) Raisins were a satisfactory substitute. (188) The washable gingham apron shown in Figure 156 must not have been considered one to be worn only for work, because it had decorative hand stitching.

From the evidence found during this period of study, it appears that the sisters in the midwestern part of the United States retained the apron after laying aside the cape, and that the sisters in the eastern part of the United States retained the dress cape longer than the apron. The demise of the apron as a part of the identifying garb of a sister as a member in the church has been almost completed. Very few, if any, sisters wore matching half aprons over their plain dresses to church on Sunday in 1970.

Shawls and Capes. A few sisters may have worn cloaks during the early part of the nineteenth century. Shawls and capes were adopted by midcentury. The first mention of wraps for the sisters in the minutes of Annual Meeting

102

Figure 150. Knee Length Apron,
Malinda Weaver, c. 1875.

Figure 151. White Apron, Malinda Royer
Bollinger, 1885.

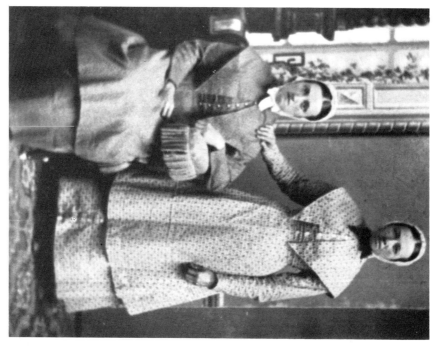

Figure 152. Dress, Apron, and Cape of Matching Fabric,
c. 1890.

Figure 153. Pleated Apron of Brown Worsted.

Figure 154. Gathered Apron of Black Sateen.

Figure 155. Apron With Decorative Tucks and Lace.

Figure 156. Gingham Apron With Embroidery.

was found in the all-inclusive Article 27 of 1866. The departure from the wearing of shawls and capes by the sisters in the church brought concern. The wearing of overcoats by the sisters was considered as conformity to the fashions of the world and therefore was prohibited. (90:313) The type of coat mentioned was clarified in Article 19 of 1881. (91:399) The sisters were given the privilege of wearing plain overcoats. The only other mention of wraps was in regard to riding habits. Sisters were advised to avoid such "superfluities" in Article 1 for 1889. (91:496)

The wearing of shawls was fashionable during the Victorian era, 1830 to 1900. The sisters in the church usually wore plain-colored shawls or patterned ones in muted shades. All the shawls that were examined during this study had fringe, usually an integral part of the shawl rather than an addition. High quality wool gave these shawls an excellent hand, fine draping qualities, and lightness in weight. After lying in a chest all week, they could be worn on Sunday without pressing. Three types were commonly worn: light-weight summer shawls, heavier winter shawls, and double shawls for extremely cold weather.

Early shawls were hand woven in the home; later ones were made commercially. The 1868 wedding portrait of Elizabeth Tully Miller shows her wearing an unusual shawl. (Figure 116) A medium-weight worsted shawl is shown in Figure 157. A shawl of similar weight is shown in Figure 158. This two-toned gray shawl, made on a Jacquard loom, showed the pattern on the opposite side in a reverse color combination. The present owner thought that this shawl was made at the Test Woolen Mill near Hagerstown, Indiana, in about 1880. The heavier woolen shawl shown in Figure 159 was commercially made also, since it was of a Jacquard pattern in three colors: brown, beige, and orange.

Double shawls were very large rectangular shawls made of moderately heavy woolen yarns. They were folded in two ways. In the first method the shawl was folded in half to form

a square, then on the diagonal to form a triangle, before being thrown about the shoulders. In the second method the shawl was folded in half, then the folded edge was turned down again. (205) This second fold was worn at the neck, permitting the shoulders to be protected with four thicknesses of fabric. An extra large double shawl is shown in Figure 160A. It measured 120 inches by 94 inches and was of medium-weight charcoal wool yarn. The owner folded this shawl in the second manner just described and threw it over her shoulders as shown in Figure 160B. One sister told the author that she remembered seeing her grandmother weave a shawl of this type. (194)

The black cashmere summer shawl shown in Figure 161 was a square measuring 62 inches on each side. It was folded diagonally before being thrown over the shoulders. Apparently two shawls were worn on a snowy day in 1942 by the sister shown in Figure 162. The light weight shawl without fringe was thrown over a heavier one. A few sisters wore light-colored shawls in summer. One sister was known to have had an imported paisley shawl. (203) The shawl shown in Figure 163 was originally white silk pongee. This sister dyed it brown to give a more somber appearance for Sunday wear. (185)

Some sisters wore capes instead of shawls during inclement weather. They varied in length from mere shoulder capes to hip and ankle length capes. All of those examined were black in color, made of wool, and lined. The long capes were made commercially. The shoulder cape shown in Figure 164 was worn in the 1890's. It was cut in a circular fashion and therefore was seamless. The neckline was finished with a straight band. The fabric was a wool brocade; the lining, a cotton sateen. A light-colored cape of similar style was thrown over the bride's arm for the wedding picture taken about 1896. It was finished at the neckline by means of a pleated double-ruffle of ribbon. The ends of the ribbon were left long enough to tie. (Figure 165)

Figure 160A. Plaid Double Shawl of Gray Wool.

Figure 159. Reversible Three-Color Winter Shawl.

Figure 158. Floral-Patterned Gray Summer Shawl.

Figure 157. Reversible Medium-Weight Plaid Shawl.

Figure 160B. Manner of Wearing a Double Shawl.

Figure 161. Manner of Wearing a Summer Shawl.

Figure 162. Shawl, Ella Young Ober, 1942.

Figure 163. Beige Silk Shawl, Mary McClellan, c. 1905.

Figure 164. Black Patterned Shoulder Cape, c. 1895.

Figure 165. Wedding Shoulder Cape, c. 1896.

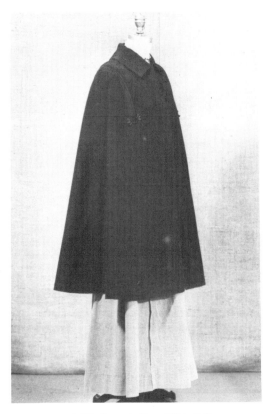

Figure 166. Hip Length Cape With Collar.

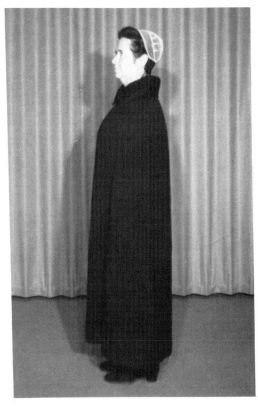

Figure 167. Ankle Length Cape of Wool Gabardine.

The finger-length cape shown in Figure 166 was made of such firm fabric that the front edge of the garment and facing were stitched together without being turned in for a seam. A bias strip of cotton sateen was used to bind the edge of the collar and for a decorative detail along the front. This strip was held in place by multiple rows of machine stitching. The full length cape shown in Figure 167 was purchased in Philadelphia. It was made of black wool gabardine, lined in satin, and fastened at the neck with a button and loop. The shaping at the shoulder was produced by an interesting arrangement of darts and dart tucks. No sisters were observed during this investigation wearing capes signifying membership in the church.

After 1900 young sisters gradually adopted conservative styles of fashionable coats. By purchasing them at marked down prices from a local dry goods store and retaining them for several years, they were out of fashion. Thus they were not criticized for wearing them. (200) However coats did not signify church membership.

Other Items of Apparel. The remainder of the outer clothing and accessory items worn by the sisters in the church differed very little from that worn by women in general throughout the nineteenth century and early part of the twentieth century. No rulings were found in the minutes of Annual Meeting regarding shoes and stockings and other accessory items. Conservative selections were made in order that these items might be in agreement in color and detail with the prescribed items. Only ostentation was objectionable.

Knitting stockings was a domestic art that a girl learned early in life during the nineteenth century. One sister said that she knitted her first pair of stockings at age twelve. (196) Tubular knitting required the manipulation of four double-pointed needles. The knitting of a stocking was more than a day's work along with other household duties. At the latter part of this century stocking yarn was purchased, rather than being spun at home. Although most stockings were black, one pair of hand-knitted, white cotton stockings was located by the investigator. They featured a well-turned heel, a full-fashioned leg, and a half-inch of ribbing at the top. (Figure 168)

The sisters continued to wear black stockings in the twentieth century. They were purchased from the local dry goods store. Stockings selected after 1900 included wool or cotton; after 1920, cotton or rayon; after 1950, nylon. A pair of black rayon stockings is shown in Figure 169. Although the majority of the sisters wore black stockings, a few sisters selected slate gray or dark beige stockings after 1920.

Shoes were a prized item on the frontier, and one pair often sufficed for all occasions. However, even one pair was not always available to sisters in less favorable circumstances. In 1876, one sister wrote that she had gone barefooted all summer because she was without means to buy shoes. (177) Another sister gathered bark in the woods to sell to a local tanner. With the money she received, she bought a pair of shoes and a dress in order to be able to join the church. (196)

Shoes worn by the sisters in the early part of the twentieth century were high enough to cover the ankle and were fastened by either laces or buttons. A pair of high top shoes featuring eleven buttons and patent leather toes is shown in Figure 170. Pointed-toed shoes were popular in the second decade. They were made of either black or brown leather. Those shown in Figure 171 were laced. Buttoning shoes was a bit difficult and a time consuming task. The button hook shown in Figure 172 was complimentary from a local dry goods store upon purchasing a pair of shoes.

Mittens and gloves were either knitted at home or purchased. Those shown in Figure 173 were made commercially. They were of double construction; the inside layer was of wool yarn and the outside layer of slack-twisted knitting silk.

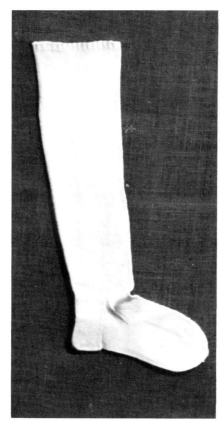

Figure 168. White Hand-Knitted Cotton Stocking.

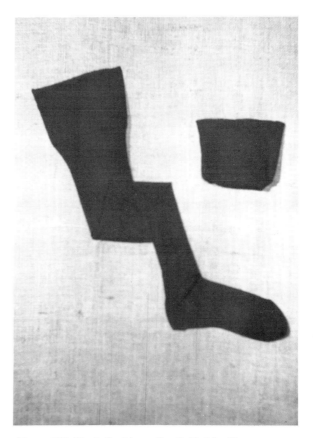

Figure 169. Black Stockings, One Folded for Storage.

Figure 170. Buttoned Shoes With Patent Trimming.

Figure 171. Laced Shoes With Pointed Toes.

110

Figure 172. Shoe Button Hook.

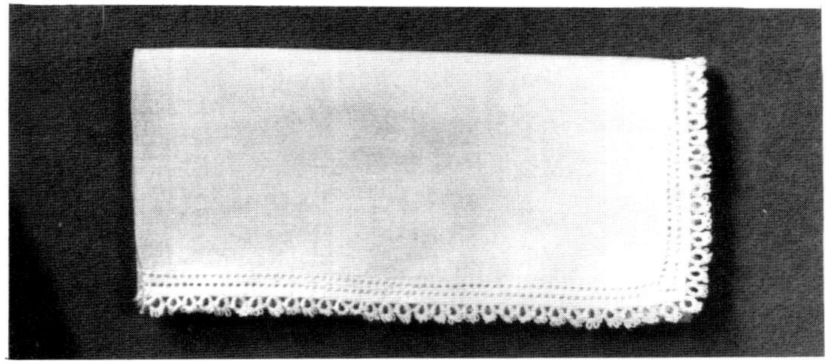

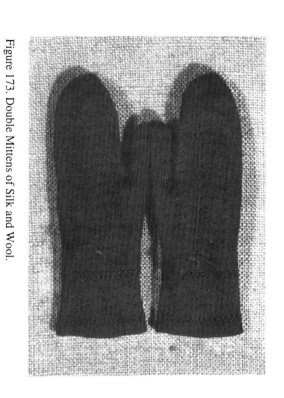

Figure 173. Double Mittens of Silk and Wool.

Figure 174. White Linen Handkerchief With Tating.

Figure 175. Purse With Lyre Clasp, c. 1900.

Handkerchiefs bought at the dry goods store were usually of white cotton. Sometimes they were hem-stitched, monogrammed, or embroidered with a small floral motif. Often they were folded in eight parts during ironing, as shown in Figure 174.

In the nineteenth century purses were small enough to be carried on the person. A black leather purse with lyre-shaped spring clasp is shown in Figure 175. Until the twentieth century a pocket on the apron, in the skirt of the dress, or on the petticoat sufficed to carry personal items. With the demise of the apron and the full-skirted dress it became necessary for sisters to carry a handbag. No one particular style was found as customarily used. Usually those purchased were made of inexpensive black leather or an imitation leather. The cap, if not worn daily, was carried to church in the handbag.

Jewelry. Inexpensive costume jewelry for women did not become a fashion item until the twentieth century. The jewelry worn in the nineteenth century was either an heirloom, a gift, or purchased at a price. Jewelry was objected to by the church for two reasons. It smacked of pride and ostentation, and the money spent for it could have been used more profitably.

The previous discussion concerning the wearing of gold by the brethren applied to the sisters as well. However, a few articles in the Annual Meeting minutes referred only to the sisters. A common practice of the brethren and sisters was to attend the communion services of neighboring churches. A query came before the Annual Meeting of 1853, as Article 8, asking whether visiting sisters wearing earrings and jewels could be excluded from communion. The decision was that the host church had the right to counsel with them and to exclude them if they refused to remove such items. (90:170)

Even though children were not members of the church they were to be dressed modestly and not after the fashions of the world. Accord-

ing to Article 10 of the minutes of 1857, the brethren, and especially the ministering brethren, were not to adorn their children with earrings, breast pins, finger rings, or other jewelry. (90:204)

After 1900 some parents gave their daughters watches upon graduation from high school. In accordance with church ruling the monogrammed watch shown in Figure 176 had a silver case rather than gold. A watch of this type was worn on a long black ribbon, a silk cord, or a silver chain about the neck. It was long enough to permit the watch to be tucked under the belt or inside the skirtband of a two-piece dress. (Figure 177)

Early in the nineteenth century nose glasses became fashionable. However, they were accepted by only a very few young sisters in the church. Despite church rulings one sister had a pair of gold-framed nose glasses in 1915. (Figure 178) Older sisters continued to wear the style of spectacles worn in the previous century. (Figure 179) According to an advertisement in *The Gospel Messenger* during 1898, nickel-plated frames with straight temple pieces could be purchased for one dollar by mail. Lenses were selected by having the customer send his age and a sample of the smallest print which he could read when holding the print twelve to fourteen inches from the eyes. (106:416)

In 1970 only a few sisters refrain from wearing brooches, beads, earrings, wristwatches, wedding bands and other rings. Some sisters consider these items inappropriate with their plain dresses.

Graveclothes. During the early part of the nineteenth century a sister was buried in a winding sheet. Later in the century either a white shroud was used (197) or one or two sisters in the local congregation made a special dress. (170) After the turn of the century many sisters were buried in their best clothing. Some sisters made certain that they had an appropriate black dress on hand in the event of such an occasion. After 1911 sisters who either wore the cap and

Figure 176. Watch With Engraved Silver Case.

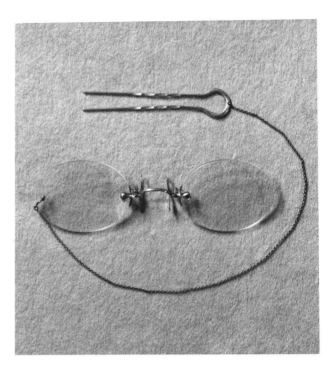

Figure 178. Nose Glasses With Gold Frames.

Figure 177. Manner of Wearing a Pendant Watch.

Figure 179. Spectacles, Elizabeth Reiff Royer, 1904.

plain dress, or cap and a fashionable dress of a simple style, were buried in the same. Bonnets were not used for burial; therefore some were available for study by this investigator.

The items of clothing which remained after the death of a sister were given to other sisters within the church. (171) Clothing was considered too personal to be sold at public auction. Plain clothing was not desired by the general public. Other items of apparel which did not signify church membership were retained by a family member, given to any person in need, or given to church relief programs and other charitable agencies.

Degrees of Conformity in Brethren Dress

No record was kept as to the percentage of the membership who adhered to the prescribed mode of dress. Therefore the following assumptions have been made by the author. The percentage of the membership adhering to the prescribed mode of dress varied with time, locale, and age of the person. At no time was there complete conformity. The degree of conformity varied from a large majority in some churches to a slight minority in others. Even with the emphasis placed upon dress in the nineteenth century, it remained a secondary issue to other issues found in the minutes of Annual Meeting. The degree of conformity was less than that perceived by more recent members reviewing their heritage. (204)

The degree of conformity in the dress of the brethren and the sisters was found to be more apparent in photographs which show more than one person. Photographs were located which show the dress at various periods of time, in various locales, before and after membership, and for various age groups. The photographs shown in Figures 180 through 207 have been grouped in the following manner: those showing the dress of a group of brethren and a group of sisters, those showing the dress of married couples and family groups, and those showing the dress of members in attendance at Annual Meeting, a Brethren college, or a local church.

Dress of Brethren

The degree of conformity achieved among the brethren is shown in a photograph of the faculty of Mount Morris College, Mount Morris, Illinois, in 1886. (Figure 180) The older staff members on the front row all conformed to the order of dress prescribed at that time. A young brother on the back row wore the clerical collar, but not the beard. The three persons remaining may not have been members of the church, although they were hired to teach at the college.

Uniformity is noted in the cut of the collars on the coats worn by members of the General Sunday School Board, representing the entire Brotherhood in 1911. (Figure 181) However, differences were noted in the cut of the remainder of the coats. Some of these brethren were wearing frock coats and others, sack coats. Some were wearing beards, with or without mustaches, whereas others were clean-shaven. Variations in the manner of wearing the beard are also found in Figure 182. Variations are also noted in the style of hats and overcoats worn by this group of brethren at Asheville, North Carolina, in 1913.

Past-moderators of Annual Meeting in attendance in 1944 are shown in Figure 183. Only four of these brethren were wearing beards. Only three were wearing clerical coats. The remainder wore coats with rolling collars and lapels and either bow ties or four-in-hand ties. The four brethren wearing beards are deceased, completing the demise of Brethren dress among these past-moderators.

Dress of Sisters

The degree of conformity achieved among the sisters can be observed in Figure 184. With one exception, all were wearing caps with black ties. All were wearing dresses featuring tightly-fitted bodices, long sleeves, and long skirts. Differ-

114

Figure 180. Faculty of Mount Morris College, Mount Morris, Illinois, Wearing the Prescribed Dress, 1886.

Figure 181. Various Hair Styles and Clerical Coats, General Sunday School Board, c. 1911.

Figure 182. Outer Wraps Worn by the Brethren, c. 1913.

Figure 183. Variety in Dress, Past-Moderators in Attendance at Annual Meeting, 1944.

Figure 184. Sisters Living Near Mount Morris, Illinois, Wearing the Prescribed Dress, c. 1891.

Figure 185. Contrasting Dress of Pupils in a Local Sunday School Class, c. 1918.

ences can be observed only in decorative detail of the dresses. Two sisters were wearing dresses of a lighter color, typical of the 1890's. None were wearing either dress capes or aprons. This picture shows the prescribed dress of that time for an ideal group of sisters, rather than what may have been the real situation. These members were either sisters or first cousins to each other and lived in or near Mount Morris, Illinois. The picture was taken about 1891 at the request of D.L. Miller, who had just returned from a visit to the Scandinavian mission. The picture was sent to the mission to show the sisters there how sisters dress in America.

A Sunday school class taught by Priscilla Neher, about 1918, at the Walnut Church in northern Indiana, is shown in Figure 185. The caps and bonnets of the sisters contrast with the hats of nonmembers in the class. The coats and shoes reflect the fashions of the day and were not a part of the distinctive dress of the church at that time.

Members of the Ladies Aid Society of the Pine Creek Church in northern Indiana in 1949 are shown in Figure 186. Meetings were held on a week day. At the time the photograph was taken, no sister was wearing a cap. However, they put on their caps when grace was offered for the noon meal. The majority of these sisters had long hair. This is the only aspect of the prescribed dress observable in the photograph.

Dress of Family Groups

The photographs in Figures 187 through 189 were taken before and after the marriage of Bud and Martha Curwin Harshbarger of Manor Hill, Pennsylvania, in 1871. These ilustrations also contrast the dress of the nonmember and member at that time. Before membership, this brother wore his hair parted on each side of his head, a necktie, and a lapelled coat and vest. (Figure 187) After membership it appears that his hair was combed straight back, but fell into a part. (Figure 189) The necktie had been discarded.

The colored shirt with white collar was not prescribed, but indicates that some brethen wore it. As a lay member, he had not adopted the clerical coat. His bride, reared a Methodist, wore the fashionable dress of that day. (Figure 188) After joining the Brethren she adopted the cap, the plain dress and cape, and short apron worn by the sisters at that time. (Figure 189)

The couple shown in Figure 190 were married in 1866 and it was assumed that the photograph was taken soon after the wedding. Elder Edmund D. and Elizabeth Long Book were members of the Perry Congregation, Blair County, Pennsylvania. He wore a beard and an "adapted" Brethren coat. She wore a cap, neckerchief, dress cape, and apron over her fitted dress.

A longer hair style was adopted in 1890 by Galen B. Royer, of Mount Morris, Illinois. (Figure 191) It is in contrast to the shorter style worn when he was married in 1885. (Figure 23) An even longer beard is shown in Figure 25. Also he changed from a lapelled coat to a clerical coat during this time. His wife, Anna Miller Royer, continued to wear the fitted dress without the dress cape and apron. Since the picture was taken at a photographic studio, she was not wearing a cap.

Four generations were represented in a photograph taken about 1891. (Figure 192) The great-grandfather, John Emmert, wore the longer hair style of the brethren and also a beard. Also he wore an "adapted" Brethren coat and uncreased trousers and carried a cane. The grandmother wore a white cap with black ties, a long dark dress, a dress cape with the collar and edge trimmed with a contrasting texture, and probably an apron. The father wore a shorter hair style, a beard, and a soft black necktie with his lapelled coat. The son wore a dress, typical of the clothing worn by young children at that time.

The order of dress prescribed by the church was observed in the family of Jonathan Cripe, who lived near North Liberty, Indiana. The

Figure 186. Ladies Aid Society, Pine Creek Church, Indiana, 1949.

Figure 187. Bud Harshbarger Before
Membership.

Figure 188. Martha Curwin Before
Membership.

Figure 189. After Membership, Bud and Martha Curwin Harshbarger Wearing the Prescribed Dress, Huntingdon, Pennsylvania, 1871.

120

Figure 190. The Prescribed Dress as Worn by Elder Edmund D. and Elizabeth Long Book, Blair County, Pennsylvania, c. 1866.

Figure 191. Galen B. Royer Family, Mount Morris, Illinois, c. 1890.

Figure 192. Variation in Dress Worn by Great-Grandfather, Grandmother, Father (David Emmert, standing), and His Young Son, Lewis, Huntingdon, Pennsylvania, c. 1890.

family photograph shown in Figure 193 was taken about 1895. The stepmother and three daughters were dressed alike. The father wore a clerical coat as a lay member. He was elected to the ministry at a later time. In all probability the oldest son had joined the church by this time, for he wore no necktie with his lapelled coat. The two younger sons would not likely have been baptized.

The family of Dennis W. Rupel, of Walkerton, Indiana, is shown in Figure 194. As deacon and deaconess, the parents wore the prescribed order of dress. The second son was a minister and wore the beard and clerical coat. The bachelor son was a teacher in the public schools at the time and wore a bow tie with his lapelled coat. The eldest son, with mustache, and wife were not members at this time. The two maiden sisters were members. They wore white waists with black skirts on the day the photograph was taken, about 1902.

Photographs of family groups show differences in the dress worn by successive generations. A portrait of the Charles Madeira family of Elizabethtown, Pennsylvania, is shown in Figure 195. The father, mother, and oldest daughter were members of the church in 1911 and wore the prescribed dress. The father wore a beard and the clerical coat; the mother wore the cap and dress cape. The ribbon on the cap worn by the daughter was left hanging in a loop. This custom was observed by a few sisters as late as 1968. The dress of the daughter featured long sleeves, a high neck, and a fitted skirt, but not the apron or cape. The four older sons were members of the church at the time. However, each wore a lapelled coat and black bow tie. The five younger children had not yet joined the church.

The family of William H. and Elizabeth Metzger Replogle of Rossville, Indiana, is shown in Figure 196. One son, a minister and school teacher, wore the clerical coat in both capaci-

ties. The other son and father wore lapelled coats and neckties. The mother and two daughters had long hair. Since they did not wear their caps daily in 1920, they did not wear them in the photographic studio.

A family gathering of the kin of Samuel Ober, Milton Grove, York County, Pennsylvania, is shown in Figure 197. The photograph was taken in 1935. The older brethren wore beards and clerical coats; the younger brother did not. The older sisters wore caps, aprons, and capes over their dresses. Only one younger sister was wearing a cap.

Like other Brethren, Frank and Alzina Whitmer Rupel left their family home in Indiana in 1912 to live at Plain, Washington. At Pasadena, California, in 1954, as a retired minister, he continued to wear a beard. He did not wear a necktie the day this photograph was taken, although he did wear one late in life. (Figure 198) She retained her long hair, but laid aside her cap for daily wear. On Sundays she wore a hat to church, but replaced it with her cap for the service.

The form of plain dress representative of the Brethren in 1968 is worn by Aaron S. Hollinger and his wife, Nellie. (Figure 199) As deacon and deaconess at the Elizabethtown Church, in Pennsylvania, they have continued to wear plain clothing although it is no longer prescribed for membership or the deaconry. He was wearing a high-crowned black felt hat with a brim of moderate width, a sack coat with clerical collar, and no necktie. She was wearing a cap, a bonnet, and a dress cape with attached waistband over a matching dress. This plain dress featured sleeves extending below the elbow, a loosely fitted bodice, and a six-gore skirt reaching to mid-calf. The jewelry worn by this couple were cuff-links, spectacles, and watches. Their children do not dress in this manner. Therefore the plain dress of the Brethren will disappear in this family with this generation.

Figure 193. Jonathon Cripe Family, North Liberty, Indiana, Wearing the Prescribed Dress, c. 1895.

Figure 194. Dennis Rupel Family, Walkerton, Indiana, Wearing Items of the Prescribed Dress, c. 1902.

Figure 195. Charles Madeira Family, Elizabethtown, Pennsylvania, c. 1911.

Figure 196. William H. Replogle Family, Rossville, Indiana, 1920.

Figure 197. Kin of Samuel Ober, Milton Grove, Pennsylvania, 1935.

Figure 198. Frank and Alzina Whitmer Rupel, Pasadena, California, 1954.

Figure 199. Plain Dress, as Worn by Aaron S. and Nellie Hollinger, Deacon and Deaconness, Elizabethtown Church, Elizabethtown, Pennsylvaina, 1968.

Dress of Church Groups

Visitors always have been welcome to observe the communion service. In Figure 200, visitors were watching the brethren perform the rite of feetwashing, symbolizing humility and service. The fashionable coat, top hat, and clean shaven face worn by these gentlemen before 1850 were in contrast to those of the brethren. The bonnets and shawls worn by the fashionable ladies present were in contrast to plainer ones worn by the sisters, although not depicted.

The Annual Meeting was held at Ottawa, Kansas, in 1887 and 1896. It has been assumed that the photograph listed as Figure 201 was taken at the earlier meeting. The view shows the Brethren gathered around the speaker's table. The hair styles of the brethren and the caps of the sisters are visible. The uniformity of dark-colored clothing is noticeable also.

An official photograph of the Annual Meeting of 1913 held at Winona Lake, Indiana, depicted many interesting contrasts in the dress of the brethren and sisters. A detail from this photograph shows a mother and her four daughters from the Bachelor Run Church in central Indiana. (Figure 202A) The mother wore a moderately large bonnet and also a cape and apron over her dress. Her four daughters wore smaller bonnets, and no capes or aprons over their long-sleeved, floor-length dresses. The brethren shown in Figure 202B depict a variety of coat and hair styles. It has been assumed that the gentleman wearing the mustache was a visitor in the crowd.

Photographs of special groups were taken at Annual Meetings. Missionaries appointed to serve in India at the Annual Meeting of 1911 are shown in Figure 203. The brother on the left wore a sack coat and the one on the right, a frock coat. All three brethren were clean shaven and had their hair shingled. The three sisters wore bonnets typical of the time. A complaint was made concerning the sister on the front row.

It was thought that she had not been properly dressed to attend the missionary dedication service. Her father gave her money to buy a long sleeved blouse that she might appear with propriety. (148:409) A part of the missionaries dedicated at the Annual Meeting of 1919 are shown in Figure 204. Some of the brethren were wearing clerical coats and others lapelled coats with dark clerical vests. More of the sisters were wearing white dresses featuring low necklines than is shown in the previous illustration. They removed their bonnets for the picture.

Students at Brethren colleges represented the future leadership of the church. Figure 205 shows a Bible class taught by B.P. Fitzwater, about 1908, at Manchester College, North Manchester, Indiana. The brethren wore either clerical coats or lapelled coats without neckties. All had shingled hair and not one wore a beard. The sisters' light-colored waists were in contrast to the men's dark coats. Several of the sisters wore caps, but not all did. Either they had laid them aside for classes or were not members of the church.

Special occasions of a local church congregation were sometimes recorded by a photographer after 1900. The members of the Red River Church, Oklahoma, gathered for the dedicatory services of their church building on a warm day in 1908. Figure 206 shows that some of the brethren wore beards and clerical coats, but not all did. A majority of the sisters wore bonnets over their caps. The degree of conformity in their dress is presumed to be representative of local churches located west of the Mississippi River at that time. A photograph of the Zion Hill congregation near Columbiana, Ohio, was taken in December, 1970. (Figure 207) The occasion was preparatory to the dedication of this new addition to the church building. The caps worn by the sisters during the Sunday morning service remain as the only visible item of clothing signifying membership.

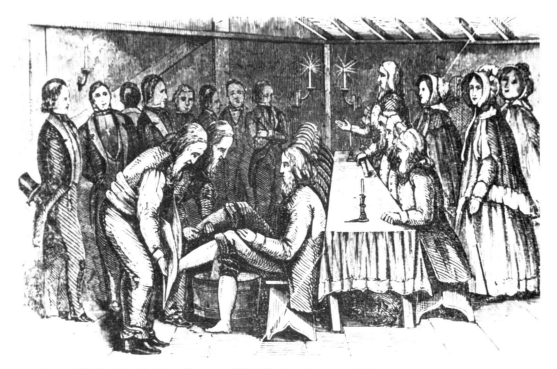

Figure 200. Fashionable Dress Contrasted With Brethren Dress, c. 1850.

Figure 201. Annual Meeting, Ottawa, Kansas, 1887 or 1896.

Figure 202B. Dress of Brethren at Annual Meeting, 1913.

Figure 202A. Dress of a Sister and Her Four Daughters at Annual Meeting, 1913.

Figure 203. Missionaries Appointed to India by Annual Meeting, 1911.

Figure 204. Some of the Missionaries Appointed to Foreign Service by Annual Meeting, 1919.

Figure 205. Students in a Bible Class Taught by P.B. Fitzwater at Manchester College, North Manchester, Indiana, c. 1908.

132

Figure 206. Dedication Day, Red River Church, Oklahoma, 1908.

Figure 207. Members of the Zion Hill Congegation, Columbiana, Ohio, Assembled in Worship in New Building, 1970.

Brethren Acceptance of Clothing Symbols of Society at Large

For the most part, the Brethren no longer separate themselves from the larger society, but have become a part of it. The situation of the church membership in 1970 regarding the wearing of the prescribed dress was analyzed as follows: a few members wear "plain dress", the style subsequent to the changes wrought with the passage of time; a somewhat larger group of members subscribe to some aspect of "plain dress", such as a cap for the sister and the absence of a necktie for a brother; and the majority of members wear no item of clothing identifying membership in the church, having adopted the fashionable attire of their socio-economic class. Discussion on the order of dress for church members has dropped from daily conversation. This author has observed no significant trend toward a new mode of dress signifying church membership.

The Brethren have adopted symbols which show their increased involvement with society at large. These symbols have been categorized by this investigator as representing four aspects in the life of the membership in 1970. The four aspects concern a membership: which belongs to the middle socio-economic class and engages in middle class occupations, which belongs to organizations promoting causes in harmony with Brethren beliefs, which pursues academic interests, and which is interested in liturgical forms of worship. Some of these symbols are shown in Figures 208 through 211.

Socio-Economic Clothing Symbols

With their rise to the middle class, the Brethren accepted the corresponding dress to designate their new status. Upon entering the business and professional world they adopted the accompanying dress. The dress suit, white shirt, polished leather shoes, and hat formerly worn only on Sunday have become the daily attire of many brethren at their jobs. The wearing of a necktie is accepted.

Although the items of clothing are less specific for the sisters, those worn for church, business, and social occasions are readily recognizable as belonging to ladies of the middle class. The majority of sisters wear a dress or suit with or without a coat, as the season demands. Recently, bifurcated garments have been adopted by younger sisters. Accessories consist of a purse, nylon hosiery, leather shoes, and perhaps gloves and hat selected within a moderate price range. Short hair is arranged in a becoming manner, sometimes with the assistance of a professional hairdresser. Wristwatches and inexpensive jewelry complete their attire. No longer is it possible to identify a sister by her clothing as a member of the church, for she does not differ in dress from a nonmember of the same age, locale, and socio-economic class.

Occupational Clothing Symbols

The dress of the Brethren minister has been discussed previously. The few brethren who entered law as a profession adopted the business suit and the customary robes associated with the bench. Many brethren and sisters as teachers wear clothing comparable to others in the profession. In the past, if a brother was a minister as well as a teacher, he wore his clerical coat in the school room. Some brethren doctors were also ministers. During the early part of the twentieth century they retained their clerical coats in the medical profession. Younger doctors adopted the business suit and necktie.

Since the Brethren were unsuccessful in establishing a nurse's training school, sisters who desire training wear the prescribed uniform of the institution they attend. (Figure 208) They wear the nurse's cap instead of a prayer cap when on duty. When off duty, they dress like other sisters. Although church publications were requested in 1909 to restrain from using pictures showing fashionable dress, pictures were

Figure 210. Membership Pins of Church Organizations.

Figure 209. WCTU Member, Elizabeth Thomas.

Figure 208. Graduate Nurse in Uniform, Roseltha Whitmer.

appointees to foreign fields of service.

Brethren entering civil service and other service occupations adopt the required uniforms. Brethren beliefs against war bring objections to military uniforms. The special Annual Meeting called in 1918 at Goshen, Indiana, urged the brethren not to enter full military duty or to wear the uniform. (45:45) In World War II those brethren who entered the various branches of the service, or as non-combatants, wore military uniforms. Others, as conscientious objectors, wore clothing appropriate in their work of national importance, whether a hospital orderly or a forest conservationist.

Organizational Clothing Symbols

Membership in various social and fraternal organizations often is designated by some item of dress or adornment. Items which designate membership in organizations with purposes which the Brethren could support are adopted by some members. A small bow of white ribbon, worn by members of the Women's Christian Temperance Union, was worn by the sister shown in Figure 209.

The General Sunday School Board apparently approved of rally day buttons, for they were advertised along with pennants and other Sunday school literature in an issue of *The Gospel Messenger* of 1917. (105:559) A contributor to the church paper in 1912 admitted that badges and pins promoted unity of feeling between members. However, he objected to their use because he felt that they led to membership in other organizations with purposes which the Brethren could not espouse. (116:643)

After 1920 various age groups were organized within the church at the national level. In the 1930's members of the Brethren Young People's Department were identified by a pin bearing the initials BYPD. (Figure 210) Members of the Brethren Service Commission giving relief in Austria following World War II were identified by pins especially made for that purpose. (Figure 210) Pins are awarded to staff members working at the General Offices of the church at Elgin, Illinois. A five-year service pin is shown in Figure 210.

Some brethren and sisters have become members of service, professional, and even fraternal organizations, and have in their possession the respective organizational jewelry. In the last few years, there has been some deviancy from the middle class dress of the adult membership on the part of Brethren youth engaged in purposeful social reform. Some wear peace symbols applied to their clothing and in the form of jewelry. However, these symbols are not distinctive to Brethren youth but are used and understood by a wider sector of the population.

Academic Regalia

As the Brethren accepted formal education, the six Brethren colleges and seminary adopted the customary academic regalia for the commencement exercises. The colorful hoods of the faculty verify academic training in graduate schools across the nation and in foreign countries. The mortar board has replaced the cap or prayer veil for the sisters on these occasions. In reviewing official portraits of past-presidents of Brethren colleges, one quickly notices which ones retained a Brethren coat and which ones were first to adopt academic robes.

Liturgical Regalia

The use of choir music in addition to congregational singing for worship services became a practice among Brethren churches in the twentieth century. An educated laity with training in vocal music made possible organized choirs. Some members favor the wearing of robes as an aid to worship in that they permit attention to be focused on the music rather than on dress of the participants. Others feel that robes make for separation between members of the choir and the audience. Many large Brethren churches have choirs which wear robes. Perhaps cost has been the greatest restraining factor in their adoption by small churches. The wearing of a cap matching the robe in fabric and color was voted out by the choir members of one church because it replaced the prayer cap. (206) Sisters in other church choirs are at liberty to wear prayer caps with robes or to participate bareheaded.

Many small churches have a volunteer choir which meets at irregular intervals. Some measure of uniformity in dress is achieved for these mixed choirs by the sisters wearing white blouses and dark skirts. The brethren then remove their coats to permit their white shirts and dark trousers to harmonize with the dress of the sisters. Some all male groups retain their lapelled coats and wear black bow ties.

Baptismal robes have become more popular in recent years, not only for the officiating minister but also for the applicant. Generally these robes are made similar in style to choir robes with less fullness to avoid any encumbrance during immersion. White percale has been a popular color and fabric choice. Baptismal robes replaced the baptismal suit of rubber formerly worn by many evangelists. Robes replaced the washable trousers and shirt or washable dress formerly worn by applicants. Shoes are slipped off at the edge of the water and the applicant enters the water in his stocking feet or barefooted. In some churches the long hair of a sister was kept out of the face and kept from getting wet by a bathing cap. In 1970 this practice is considered unnecessary because of the prevalence of hair dryers and casual hair styles.

To the world, ministers who wore the Brethren coat were looked upon as untrained farmer-preachers. Ministers who wore liturgical regalia in the pulpit represented the emphasis of Protestantism on a scholarly clergy. (193) Some Brethren take offense at the practice of wearing clerical and academic robes in the pulpit. They consider the minister to be on the same plane as the laity. (145:11) Others feel that ministers who wear robes are aping after more fashionable ministers. (158:26) A rebuttal appeared in the *Messenger* for 1969. The author perceived the minister's robe as a tool to promote worship because it is a symbol of simplicity and a symbol of a profession for which a man is dedicated to God and obligated to other men. (90:35) Perhaps the use of robes in the church was epitomized in the dedicatory service at the Annual Meeting of 1969 held at Louisville, Kentucky. While wearing their doctoral robes, a stole was passed from the retiring moderator to his successor. The act symbolized the shift in responsibility of the headship of the church to the incoming moderator. (Figure 211)

Figure 211. Wearing Academic Regalia, Past-Moderator Morley J. Mays (right) Greets Newly Elected Moderator A.G. Breidenstine. Passing of the Stole Symbolized the Transfer of Leadership of the Church of the Brethren for the Ensuing Year, 1969-1970.

Chapter 5

CHURCH POLITY CONCERNING DRESS

As the Brethren attempted to apply their beliefs to every phase of daily living and to maintain a separation from the world, their manner of dressing became an issue before the church. Deviation from a mode of dress which had come to signify membership in this religious sect was perceived as disruptive to the group. The authority for disciplining erring members was taken from the scriptures, Matthew 18 and Acts 15. The purpose of passing rules, or sumptuary laws, to regulate dress was fourfold; to carry out the directives of the scriptures, to retain the purity of the church, to maintain a spirit of unity within the church, and to save an individual from eternal perdition.

Polity in Europe, 1708-1733

The conclusion has been drawn that the Brethren in Europe, as refugees and members of a protesting religious sect, did not achieve conformity in dress and therefore did not prescribe a mode of dress for membership within the group. This investigator has assumed that there were no rules regarding dress passed by any official body of the church at that time. Commitment to the basic values held by the group on the part of the members made for simplicity in dress but not for conformity. Individual cases of deviancy would have been dealt with personally by admonishment and avoidance on the part of the other members.

Polity in America, 1719-1800

The conclusion has been drawn that the dress of the Brethren during this period identified them as immigrants of German origin, members of the lower socio-economic class and persons who led pious lives. Thus their dress differed from the dress of immigrants of different origin and from the dress of persons who dressed fashionably. A particular mode of dress did not yet signify membership in this religious group. Therefore the polity of the church during this period did not concern dress. Deviant behavior on the part of an individual member would have been cared for by other members who either admonished or shunned the deviant.

Polity in America, 1801-1970

Dress as an issue before the church gradually increased in intensity during the nineteenth century. This was due in part to a desire for greater unity within the fellowship because of schismatic elements and to greater involvement of the membership with society at large. This resulted in the official church governing body at the national level taking a stand in regard to dress. Erring members came under specific rulings of the church. Erring churches were subject to the counsel of committees appointed by the governing body.

In reviewing the minutes of the governing body, or Annual Meeting, more than one hundred entries were found concerning the issue of dress. Four types of rules were evident: those opposing ostentation in dress, symbolized in fashionable dress; those dealing with a particular hair style or item of clothing, which have already been discussed; those listing dress requirements for membership and for the holding of an office; and those dealing with protesting members or factions in a local church. Further tightening of the rules was due to irregularities in wearing the prescribed mode of dress and inconsistencies in disciplining members. The issue in its totality came before the Annual Meetings of 1898 and 1909. The decision adopted by the Annual Meeting of 1911 reaffirmed the prescribed mode of dress as the ideal, but no longer made it a test of fellowship. This decision and subsequent decisions concerning dress have remained on the minutes of Annual Meeting.

Dress Requirements of the Laity.

The Brethren attending Annual Meeting in 1804 advised against the new women's fashions promulgated by the French court. Article 9 of the minutes stated that the sight of such grieved God Almighty, the angels, and the faithful souls on earth. Members of the church and their children who followed these fashions were gratifying "the lust of the eye". Bishops, ministers, and parents were to work diligently to counteract this evil that others might deny themselves of such worldliness and be willing to join the fellowship of believers. (90:35) During the remainder of the century numerous rulings were passed against the wearing of fashionable dress. (see Table 1 in Appendix B)

At Baptism. Baptism was not to be entered into lightly by an applicant. Article 8 of the minutes of the Annual Meeting for 1837 stated that if necessary the applicant was to be instructed in the "practices peculiar to the Brethren". He was not only to affirm his faith but also to state his willingness to refrain from wearing the fashions of the world. (90:81) A reconsideration of the above article in 1886, as Article 7, gave greater specificity to the re-

straints, and added that the wearing of a cap was required of the sisters. (91:450)

A brother administering the rite of baptism who neglected his duty to teach nonconformity in dress was subject to the authority of Annual Meeting, as stated in Article 63 of the minutes for 1862. (90:267) Sometimes the vows were asked of the applicant while in the water. Other ministering brethren felt it was better to take the vows before entering the water on such an emotional occasion. Members observing the rite were witnesses to the vows taken by the applicant.

As an economic measure, new members were given time to wear out the clothing they had on hand before adopting the prescribed order of dress. When this period lasted for two or three years, some members felt it was time to take the situation in hand. A query on the issue came before the Annual Meeting of 1849 as Article 25. It requested that those not in the order should be prohibited from communing.

Witness to Membership. Consistency in living the Christian life was important to the Brethren. Having professed Christ and denounced the world there was to be no return to the former manner of living. Brethren were to make their witness wherever they went. Article 9 in the minutes of the Annual Meeting of 1847 stated that a brother or sister should not have two suits of clothing, a "plain" one for church meetings and a "fashionable" one for secular occasions. (90:120)

Neither were the sisters to wear fashionable dresses for meetings held during the day at Annual Meeting and then change to plainer dresses for the communion service in the evening. If this happened, the answer given to Article 6, in 1858, permitted these sisters to commune, but the elder of their home congregation was to be informed. He was to admonish the offending sisters and take further action if they remained disobedient. (90:210)

In turn every lay member, not just the ministering brethren, had the privilege and duty to admonish any other lay member or official who had drifted from the plain order of dress prescribed by the church. According to Article 38, passed by the Annual Meeting of 1862, such a warning was to be given in a spirit of meekness and love. (90:262)

According to Article 4, of the minutes of 1889, members were not to take part in drama productions of any kind. The answer for the query was prepared at district meeting by the First District of West Virginia. Masquerade costumes were considered out of order, according to I Corinthians 10:7. (91:496)

All who wore the order of dress prescribed by the church were to bear witness to their faith and vice versa. However, at the Annual Meeting of 1889, an imposter appeared in one of the tents on the grounds. Upon being questioned, it became obvious that he didn't know the "proper" answers that any Brethren would know. This wolf in sheep's clothing was really a man in the plain dress of a sister. (135:574)

Test of Fellowship. Any member who had been admonished three times for not dressing in the order of the church was not to be held in full fellowship, according to Article 2, in 1817. (90:52) The disciplinary measure to be taken by a local church council with regard to this digressive behavior was to restrict the member from "full fellowship". This meant that he would not be saluted with the kiss of charity, nor be elected to office, nor be allowed to remain in office, nor be allowed to participate in the communion service. However, his name remained on the church roll until further action by the church council restored him to his former status or excommunicated him. Members who rejected the council of the church were to be dealt with according to Matthew 18. According to this scripture, after all attempts at reconciliation on the part of individuals and the church

failed, the offender was to be treated "as an heathen man and a publican". Then his name was struck from the membership roll, and he was lost to eternal perdition, or until such time as he made confession and was restored by action of the same church in council. This same position regarding dress was reaffirmed by the Annual Meetings of 1822, 1866, and 1871.

Letters of Membership. Transference of membership from one church to the other was granted at the request of the individual via the council meeting of his local congregation. With the consent of the members present that the applicant was a member in good standing, and that there were no grievances between him and another member, the letter was signed by the clerk and handed to the individual. The letter, or certificate, was then presented to the clerk of the next church and read at its next council meeting for acceptance or rejection.

Some members sometimes took advantage of a situation by placing their letters in a neighboring church which was more lenient with regard to dress. The first query on the agenda for the Annual Meeting of 1881 gave permission for a church to reject a letter if the applicant was not dressed in the order. (91:390) Also authorities of the district in which a church was located which granted an improper letter could take disciplinary action against that church.

The Annual Meeting of 1923 received two queries concerning the granting and receiving of letters. A committee was appointed and a report was presented the next year. Because of inconsistencies in the demands of various congregations regarding dress, an objection to the granting of a letter if due only to irregularities in dress, could be stated on the back of the letter. (87:12) Upon receiving a letter with objections stated on the back, the elder presented it with the objections to the congregation convened in council for acceptance or rejection. If the letter were rejected, the two congregations involved were to adjust the case. (77:56) In 1931 the Annual Meeting made a restatement of the 1926 decision regarding the granting and receiving of letters of membership. Although the sentiment was the same as the previous report, there was no specific mention of dress in the new membership letter adopted. (78:74)

Students attending Brethren colleges were expected to transfer their letter of membership to the host church during the school year. Others who joined the church while attending college became members of the host church. Sometimes the host church was perceived by the home churches as being too lenient with regard to dress. In turn the home churches were perceived by the host church as being too lenient. One contributor to *The Gospel Messenger* proposed that local congregations assist the colleges by not permitting members to wear garments in the home church that were not permitted at school. Furthermore, parents were to assist the administrators of the colleges in retaining plain dress by censoring what went into college bound trunks. (166:520)

Dress Requirements of Officiants.

Fulfilling the duties of office ranged from a single occasion to a lifetime commitment. The occasions ranged from such less-demanding tasks as being a pallbearer at a funeral to years of service as a minister or a missionary. At times duties overlapped and increased the demands made on an individual and his influence in the group.

Pallbearers. The Annual Meeting of 1900 advised in Article 13 that Brethren who served as pallbearers were not to follow the custom of wearing badges and white gloves. (97:721) The holding of a funeral service for a nonmember in the community at a convenient Brethren church house had long been a privilege granted to the family of the deceased. However, if the service was to include the regalia customarily used for a member of a secret order, the privi-

lege was to be withheld, according to Article 9 of the minutes for 1903. (91:781)

Sunday School Teachers and Officers. Sunday school teachers and officers were required to dress in the order, as recorded in the council meeting minutes for one local church. (100) The General Sunday School Committee of the brotherhood was requested by Article 8, 1899, to select only teachers who were dressed in the order to teach at the Sunday school sessions at Annual Meeting. (91:357)

Teachers in Brethren Colleges. Members of the church who were privileged to attend Brethren colleges were looked upon with favor, but those who served on the faculty received even greater commendation. In turn they were expected to uphold the position of the church in all matters, including the order of dress. Students and faculty members at Salem College, Bourbon, Indiana, were required to dress in the order of the church, according to Article 27, of the minutes of the Annual Meeting for 1871. (90:367)

By the adoption of a report, recorded in the minutes of 1893, it became the duty of each committee of elders assigned to visit the colleges to see that efforts were made on the part of the administration to maintain plainness of dress among the faculty as well as the student body. (91:576) Methods included private admonitions, chapel talks (173), and disciplinary action. The degree of conformity to the order of dress differed at the various Brethren colleges as noted in the reports of the visiting committees reporting to the Annual Meeting of 1896. (91:646)

Delegates. The ruling of Annual Meeting in 1876 presented a problem to the moderator. Speakers from the floor were to be given the privilege of addressing the audience only if they were dressed in the order of the church. Thus it was necessary for the moderator not only to see that the business was conducted fairly and efficiently, but also to evaluate the dress of those seeking the privilege to speak. The progressive element in the church objected vehemently to the passage of Article 8 that year (90:415), and also to a similar ruling found in Article 16 in 1881. (62:46) With the requirement that all delegates to be seated at district meetings and Annual Meetings be dressed in the order, the progressive element was left out. Since they no longer dressed in the order of the church, they could not speak, and therefore were without representation. The debate became heated, and Annual Meeting was accused of being a tyrant and of having strayed from biblical principles, the teachings of Alexander Mack, the example of the old Brethren in the church, and the guidance of local church fathers of thirty years ago. (62:46) The total situation was not reconciled, and the progressive element organized as a separate body the next year.

Although it did not change the principle, an attempt was made to right the situation with the passage of Article 17 at the same meeting in 1881. (91:399) State districts were then requested to send to Annual Meeting only delegates who dressed in the order. Article 7 in 1894 imposed the regulation further by requiring local churches to send to district meeting only delegates who dressed in the order. (91:600) Some churches were not represented at these meetings because delegates, upon being informed by the credentials committee about the rulings regarded dress, simply went home before the business session started. Sisters were granted the privilege of being sent as delegates if they were exemplary members and dressed in the order, according the Article 5, in 1899. (67:91)

By action of the Annual Meeting of 1904, a committee was appointed to draw up a credential blank giving the requirements for delegates. (91:794) The blank was adopted in 1905. A delegate who placed his signature on the blank declared among other things that he did not wear gold and defended plain dress and nonconformity to the world. (91:808)

Members of the credentials committee of the Annual Meeting of 1918 found it necessary to reproach delegates who appeared before them wearing a coat with rolling collar and necktie. To avoid offending the delegate by reminding him of the rules, they felt that churches should send only delegates who dressed in the order. (144:471) An influential member took the opposite position in an article he wrote for *The Gospel Messenger* in 1920. He stated that Annual Meeting had a right to control the private lives of the members in regard to moral issues. However, he favored sending the most capable delegate regardless of the clothing he wore. (157:626) This opinion was not upheld by the District Meeting of Southern Pennsylvania that same year. It recommended that delegates sent to Sunday school conventions and interdenominational meetings should wear the prescribed dress. (96:12)

Speakers. By action of the Annual Meeting of 1863, Article 8, the brethren of a local congregation were not to invite speakers from other congregations without the consent of the presiding elder. (90:271) Usually he knew these men and knew whether they dressed in the order. Nor were local churches to permit speakers going out from their midst who were not so dressed, according to Article 33 for 1871. (90:368) Each local church was to guard against brethren traveling as evangelists who did not defend the order of dress by both precept and example. Those who digressed were to be called into account by the local church assembled in council.

Apparently the enthusiasm for foreign mission work got out of hand at the Annual Meeting of 1885, for the next year a query was brought to the meeting by the Committee on Arrangements. Article 3 requested that any sister who appeared on the platform was to wear the approved modest head covering rather than an "objectionable head-dress and other disapproved articles of dress". (63:12) In 1918 Annual Meeting granted the request that all members who appeared on programs at district meetings and Annual Meetings should be in sympathy and conform to the order of dress. The adopted minute pointed out the great influence of speakers upon the laity. (74:84)

Ministering Brethren. Compliance with the rules of Annual Meeting was especially important for deacons, ministers, and elders. They were responsible not only for their own conduct, but the conduct of others, as stated in Article 8, 1864. (90:280) A resolution to enforce plainness of dress upon all officers and ministers in the church was adopted in 1866, under Article 47. (90:317) Offenders were subject to being brought under the counsel of the church. Article 4 of the next year requested that the word "advise" be substituted for "enforce", but the request was not granted. (90:321)

Brethren were elected to the office of deacon and various degrees of ministry by action of the local church in council. Members were instructed by the Annual Meeting of 1873, Article 18, not to vote for candidates who did not conform to the order. (172) Article 3 of the minutes for 1899 granted a local church the right to withhold advancement in the ministry from those who did not conform in dress. (91:697) The Annual Meeting of 1870 in Article 21 granted a local church the authority to remove from office a minister who taught against the order of the church, thus granting license in dress. (90:289) According to Article 5, 1878, it was the duty of the local church to call in adjoining elders to carry out the disciplining of ministering brethren. (91:357) If necessary, these elders in turn could request a committee from Annual Meeting to either gain reconciliation or removal. Article 18 in 1882 reaffirmed this position. (91:411)

Ministers were elected to eldership by action of the elders body of a given district. For this advancement the applicant had to promise to comply with the order of dress, as required by Article 31, 1877. (91:354) Elders who did not conform were not to be granted the privilege of passing the sacraments during the communion service, according to Article 14, 1878. (91:359) Nor was an elder to serve a sister who wore a hat at the table, Article 16, 1877. (91:349) Elders who did not expel sisters for wearing hats were to be "dealt with as transgressors", as stated in Article 21, 1881. (91:399)

Authority of Official Bodies Regarding Dress

The authority for a governing body within the church was taken from the New Testament. The rules of Annual Meeting were based on the scriptures and were not of human design. Therefore the rules of Annual Meeting were considered to be obligatory and were to be made a test of fellowship until such time as changes were made, according to Article 1 in 1860. (91:195) Brethren differing in opinion were not to teach contrary to the rules, but were to bring the matter before the church for reconsideration. (91:114) Changes were to be made in the rules only if they brought practice in closer harmony with the Gospel, according to Article 18 in 1880. (91:377) If the scriptures were silent on an issue, then Annual Meeting could advise only and not rule. (91:239)

The authority of the church to require an order of dress was called directly into question in 1870. Article 18 read:

> How is it considered for members to argue that the old order of the brethren in wearing a plain garment is the tradition of men, and say there is no scripture for such order?
>
> Answer: We consider it wrong for members to do so, and if they persist in such a course they should be admonished. (90:356)

One opinion on the former decisions regarding dress by Annual Meeting appeared in *The Gospel Messenger* in 1909. "Whatever may be said of the minutes in other respects, they certainly do hang together on the subject of nonconformity to the world in dress." (133:821) No doubt there was greater consistency in the minutes than in the practice by the membership.

Local Church Council Meetings. The membership gathered in council was the basis of all church government. Each member in good standing had a right to speak and to vote. The group as a whole held the right to accept or reject a member, to commend or discipline a member, and to elect a member to or remove from office. The laity of a local church could bring pressure to bear upon a presiding elder who permitted "pride" in the church. The answer given to Article 3 in 1872, stated that the negligent elder was to be admonished before further action was taken by the council. (57:9)

The voice of the majority of the membership ruled unless the minority could prove that the majority had sidestepped the authority of the scriptures and the decisions of Annual Meeting. If the majority within a church was opposed to the requirement of wearing plain dress, the minority was given direction on how to handle the situation in Article 4 of 1882. (91:580) Although a local church had the right to appeal to higher bodies for assistance in settling difficulties, it could not negate their decisions.

By 1870 the deacons and ministering brethren of a local congregation formed an official body in directing the affairs of the group. They were expected to reach a consensus on each item of business presented to the local congregation. They were expected to support and admonish each other, even on matters of dress. (91:372)

District Elders Body. All elders of one district formed an official body. It had only the power to make recommendations to the delegate body assembled at district meeting. However, it was to take action regarding members of its own body who did not conform to the order of dress. (95:34) In 1900 the District of Eastern Pennsylvania petitioned Standing Committee for immediate action to help stay the advance of worldly fashions within the churches of the district. Irregularities had been caused by the acceptance of new members who did not conform to the order of dress, and by the organizing of new churches which ignored the rules. (95:15)

Standing Committee and Subcommittees. Only elders dressed in the order of the church were eligible to serve on Standing Committee. It appears that there was greater leniency at some times than others. The editor of the official church paper noted the dilemma of the Standing Committee of 1912. Elected members who lacked conformity in this matter could not be seated without the consent of those who did. The reason stated for this dilemma was that districts had been careless about ordaining elders who refused to wear the beard. If a beardless elder were not seated, a church district was left without representation. (111:380) The only solution was to abide by the decisions of Annual Meeting when ordaining elders.

Committees appointed by Annual Meeting were for the purpose of studying a paper, settling difficulties in a local church, making visitations to colleges and mission field, or promoting a special work of the church. Committee members were selected from the membership of Standing Committee or the elders body of a district. No church was free of the possibility of having the need to call a committee for disciplinary reasons. A committee was sent to the Germantown and Philadelphia Churches in 1868, (90:339), and again to the Philadelphia Church in 1875. It had been reported that a majority of the membership in the Philadelphia

Church was out of order. Dress was included as the last of nine irregularities listed in the report of the committee. Although the report was rejected by the local church, it was accepted by the Annual Meeting of 1876. (60:60+) This church was ahead of its time, for many churches have since adopted the practices objected to by the committee, and at that time would have been subjected to the same discipline.

Apparently matters did not improve, for the District of Southern Illinois requested that the Annual Meeting of 1881, in Article 5, not send representatives on committees who did not dress in the order of the church. (91:397) West reported in 1880 that there were calls for twenty-one committees, but only fifteen were sent. Forty committees were needed in 1881 to settle existing difficulties. (62:30)

The General Mission Board was under the direction of Annual Meeting. It was to see that every person appointed to serve at home and on foreign mission fields complied with the order of dress. All applicants were required to be willing to defend the "principles of the Gospel and the doctrines and peculiarities of the church", according to Article 6 of the minutes of Annual Meeting for 1890. (91:615) All book agents under appointment by the Book and Tract Committee were to comply also, as stated in Article 12, 1893.

A concise doctrinal statement of the beliefs of the Brethren with scriptural citation became known as *The Brethren's Card*. (98) After revision it was presented to the Annual Meeting of 1923 for adoption. However, the Annual Meeting referred it to the Tract Examining Committee rather than adopt it lest it become a creed. Two points regarding dress were included in this statement: that members should avoid extravagant and immodest dress and should appear at worship services dressed according to I Corinthians 11. The card was distributed freely in established churches and by evangelists and teachers working in areas unacquainted with the Brethren.

The Brethren Publishing House, as an arm of the church, was subject to the decisions of Annual Meeting. Illustrations used in church publications were subject to the scrutiny of members concerned with retaining the order of dress. A motion to prohibit the use of pictures of members who did not conform to the order of dress was passed by the Annual Meeting of 1909. (69:88) The editors admitted that sometimes they were at a loss to know whether the persons depicted were members. Furthermore publishers of private publications did not always adhere to the rules of the church.

Major Decisions Regarding Dress by Annual Meeting

Even though the schisms in the church during the 1880's had drawn off progressive and conservative factions within the membership, diverse opinions still remained. There were members who feared another division within the church, this time over the issue of dress. Four positions were taken by the membership: that the loss of the order of dress would result in practices which no longer adhered to the principles of modesty and plain dressing as taught by the New Testament, regardless of the rules of Annual Meeting; that the adopted order of dress was a means of retaining these principles which had been ascribed to in the decisions of Annual Meeting and should not be changed until Annual Meeting reversed them; that the teachings of the New Testament could conscientiously be carried out in simple dress, though not prescribed; and that the church should place no restrictions on a person's dress and appearance. (141:313) The future growth of the church was dependent upon a decision in regard to the dress question which would satisfy all groups. Whatever the answer was to be, it had to develop out of a discussion by the membership and be supported by the delegate body at the national level.

Decision on Dress of 1898. Inconsistencies in handling cases of discipline regarding dress caused a query to be brought before the Annual Meeting of 1897. Article 3 stated that sisters who wore hats were disfellowshiped, whereas brethren who wore many styles and fashions of the world were retained. (91:654) A committee of five brethren was appointed by Standing Committee to "devise some plan" to remove this inconsistency.

Rather than pass more rulings, the comprehensive report of the committee, adopted in 1898 as Article 3, propounded greater adherence to the position of the church on dress, greater consistency in disciplining erring members and more teaching on the matter by the ministering brethren. The adopted report read as follows:

> (1) This inconsistency exists to some slight extent, resulting from a violation of the decisions of Annual Meeting... Not more decisions, but a more intelligent understanding of the important Gospel principles of non-conformity to the world, plain dressing and plain living is what is needed.
>
> (2) We therefore beseech all elders, ministers and teachers to teach these important Scriptural doctrines earnestly, intelligently, and fully in all their charges, and to make every possible effort to carry them out,...
>
> (3) That more teaching may be done in private, elders and ministers are required to carry out fully the decisions of Annual Meeting as to pastoral visit; and the congregations shall assist in the work by giving such financial aid as circumstances may require.
>
> (4) Gospel plainness requires that the sisters attire themselves in plainly-made garments free from ornament, ruffles and all unnecessary appendages. Plain bonnets and hoods are in harmony with Gospel plainness, and are adopted as the head dress for our sisters. The brethren likewise should dress themselves in plain attire, not wearing fashionable hats and neckties, gold for adornment or other superfluities.... It is the duty of all housekeepers to see that the

> brethren and sisters are properly instructed concerning the necessity of Gospel plainness and it is also their duty to see that the order of the church, respecting plainness, is properly carried out in their respective congregations.
>
> (5) Elders who refuse and neglect to teach and enforce Gospel plainness in their respective congregations shall be reported to the elders of the District whose duty it shall be to see that the principles of nonconformity are carried out in all the churches. (91:669)

This decision became known as the dress decision of 1898, and stood until the issue was brought again before the Annual Meeting of 1909.

Decision on Dress of 1909. By 1909 it was evident that the decision on dress of 1898 was no longer acceptable to the membership as a whole. More and more articles appeared in the church paper expressing the concerns of individual members. It became evident that the dress question was an issue that would have to be dealt with by the governing body in the near future.

The elders of the District of Middle Pennsylvania set forth their views in an early issue of *The Gospel Messenger* in 1909. They felt that differences of opinion were due to the diversity of environment, occupation, family circumstance, and local church customs. Only discord would result from enforcing one mode of dress. In some churches inconsistency in disciplining members was the issue, not simplicity of dress. Efforts to maintain a mode of dress sapped the strength and spirituality of the church and lead to schism. Church unity should be sought on issues more important than dress. Adherence to a mode of dress should not be made a test of fellowship. The biblical doctrine of "plain, modest, and becoming attire should be taught as never before". (152:100)

Three queries regarding the dress question were received by the Annual Meeting of 1909 held at Harrisonburg, Virginia. They first asked Annual Meeting to deal with the inconsistencies of disciplining erring members. (69:98+) The second asked that a plan be devised which would bring harmony in the church. The last requested that Annual Meeting appoint a committee to study aspects of the issue. (69:65) During the discussion, which began in the morning business session and continued into the afternoon, over twenty persons participated in the debate, recorded in eighteen pages of the *Full Report.* (69:65+) Upon referral to Standing Committee, its recommendation was adopted by the delegate body. A vote of 289 in favor of the motion and 98 opposed exceeded the two-thirds majority required for adoption. (69:82) The adopted report read:

> In view of the fact that those queries clearly touch the vital problem of the dress question, now disturbing the peace of the Brotherhood, I move that a committee of seven faithful, intelligent, conservative brethren be appointed, to whom these papers shall be submitted, to be reported on at a coming Annual Meeting.
>
> That the committee be instructed to examine carefully and exhaustively the scriptural ground on the subject of Christian attire, that the practice of the primitive church be investigated, and the position and teaching of our own church fathers and the Minutes of our Conferences be examined, with a view of giving us a clear, concise restatement of our position on this vexed question, so that all may understand alike and be unified and dwell together as becometh children of the family of God– in love and peace and harmony.
>
> During the time the committee, so appointed, is considering the queries, the dress question shall not be considered an open one for discussion in the Messenger, but those having suggestions of a helpful character to make, are invited to write the chairman of the committee; and further, in the meantime, elders, ministers, and teachers are exhorted to teach earnestly and intelligently the scriptural doctrine of plain dressing and plain living as set forth by our Annual Meeting, so that the Church may

not depart from these principles that have been so dear to all our faithful members since she was first organized. (91:895)

The fact that Annual Meeting opened discussion on the question of dress which had been closed in 1898, showed that there was a willingness to deal with pertinent issues before the membership of the church. The editor of the church paper commented on the hopeful outlook felt in the audience after the question was sent to committee. (110:377)

Decision of Dress of 1910. The committee on dress met twice during the year and brought the following report before Annual Meeting of 1910, held at Winona Lake, Indiana. It read as follows:

> I. We examined carefully and exhaustively the scriptural ground on the subject of Christian attire and found, in all the teachings and examples of Christ and the apostles, in letter and in spirit, that the followers of Christ are to be a people separated from all worldliness, vanity, and sin... We found that the New Testament teaches:–
>
> 1. General nonconformity to the world and transformation from the world, which includes giving shape to the outward personal appearance...
> 2. Christ's followers are conformed to his image...
> 3. Christ's followers are to dress plainly and modestly...
> 4. Dress should not be extravagant...
> 5. Dress may become an abomination in the sight of God...
> 6. Garments worn for display or to attract attention are disapproved...
> 7. All Christian characteristics require modesty and plainness of the outward appearance and a corresponding meek and quiet spirit within...
>
> II. We investigated the practice of the Primitive Church, following closely the Apostolic Period, and found the Early Church Fathers exceedingly strong and

pointed in their teaching against pride and superfluity in dress...

III. We examined the position and teaching of our own Church Fathers and found a remarkable unity of teaching, that separateness from the foolish fashions of the world in dress must be maintained as taught in the New Testament.

IV. We examined the Minutes of our Conferences on dress and found that the full and unwavering purpose has been to maintain and exemplify gospel simplicity in apparel and personal appearances...

We therefore offer the following:

After a careful and prayerful investigation of the Scriptures and the writing of the Primitive Church Fathers on dress and adornment of the body, we recommend the decisions of Annual Meeting, as given in the Minutes from year to year, as the best interpretation and application of the Scriptures on nonconformity to the world in dress, in a practical way, as the rule for all the brethren and sisters in all the churches of the Brotherhood, as the means to a greater union in Christian fellowship and the simplicity of the Gospel. (79:5)

Over twenty-five brethren participated in the discussion which extended over forty-five pages of the *Full Report.* (70:120) The report had presented both biblical and historical evidence in favor of retaining the prescribed mode of dress. However, it had not presented a forthright plan to the church for unifying the various factions regarding the question of dress. The delegate body voted 361 to 135 in favor of a substitute motion to resubmit the question to a new committee which was to make a report the following year. (109:393)

The editor of the church paper commented on the six hours spent in discussion before an audience of six to eight thousand members. "We never had a fuller or freer discussion of any subject in an Annual Meeting." (109:393) Many

viewpoints were presented during the debate on the question. A decision required the best efforts of the church and time should be allowed for reaching consensus. God directed the vote of each delegate present. *The Gospel Messenger* should either be closed to discussion while the question was in committee to prevent misunderstandings, or it should be an open forum for teaching and exhortation on the matter. (70:120+)

Points of the discussion by those members favoring the adoption of the paper and retaining the order of dress followed these lines of thought. The church had a right to interpret the scriptures and make rules for its corporate body. The "uniform" promoted unity among the membership and thus strengthened the church. The divergency in dress within the church was due to a lack of self-denial on the part of the individual. The present divergency was due to a new membership not reared in the Brethren tradition. The humility and spirituality of the membership would be lost with the discarding of plain dress. The "uniform" prevented a member from entering sinful places. The "uniform" permitted a member to give service where otherwise entrance was not readily accessible. The church should take a positive stand and lead out in a campaign against worldly fashions. (70:120+)

Those members opposing the adoption of the paper and thus rejecting the prescribed mode of dress presented the following points during discussion. A prescribed "uniform" was not scriptural, and was based only on the rules of Annual Meeting. A plain and modest dress was scriptural, but no specific form should be designated. The principle of Gospel plainness did not demand uniformity in dress. The adoption of worldly dress was not a gross sin in the classification given by St. Paul. Legalism was Pharisaic, whereas the offering of love and forbearance was Christian. By adopting rules, the church was legalistic; by offering charity, it was Christian. Both Christ and the apostles wore the dress commonly worn in their day, thus prescribed dress was unnecessary to follow the example of the Master. There were inconsistencies in the disciplining of members, elders, and churches which were not in the prescribed order of dress. Each generation must deal with the dress question in its own time. (70:120+)

Decision on Dress of 1911. The minutes of the meetings of the committee bringing the report in 1911 have not been located even though they were recorded. (183) Their report was presented at the Annual Meeting of 1911, held at St. Joseph, Missouri. H.C. Early, moderator for the business session, stated in his opening remarks that in the past the Brethren had not discriminated between gospel principle and practice. God had formulated the principles and the church was to speak to their application. (71:91+)

Some members wanted the report spread on the minutes for one year, others saw no value in delaying the decision. After a lively discussion with suggestions for additions, deletions, and substitutions, which filled thirty pages of the *Full Report*, the delegate body voted to delete Section 11 of the report and adopted the remainder. The report as adopted read:

> Pursuant to the foregoing instructions "to take the whole matter under advertisement and to make a restatement" we preceded as follows:
>
> I. We examined prayerfully the scriptural grounds of Christian attire, and found that Jesus and the apostles taught honesty and simplicity of life and modesty in dress and manners.
>
> The scriptures bearing on the subject of dress and adornment are of several classes:
>
> First. Jesus condemned anxious thought for raiment (Matt. 6:25-33; Luke 12:22-31).
>
> Second. The direct teachings, such as 1 Tim. 2:9, 10; 1 Peter 3:3-5.

> Third. Teachings on nonconformity to the world in general, and that apply to dress on general principles, such as Rom. 12:1,2; 1 Cor. 10:31; 1 Peter 1:14, 15; 1 John 2:15-17.
>
> II. Investigation shows that the early Church Fathers and our own church fathers taught strongly and uniformly against pride and superfluity in dress, and constantly in favor of gospel plainness.
>
> III. The Minutes of Conference show that the Church of the Brethren has, throughout her entire history, stood firmly against the fashions of the age, and extravagance in all manner of living, and on the other hand has taught faithfully the principles of simplicity of life and personal appearance. And, furthermore, the Conference has, from time to time, adopted means and methods with the view of maintaining gospel simplicity in dress in the church body.
>
> Now, since the Gospel teaches plain and modest dress and since this is taught in the form of an obligation, without rules and methods of application further than to exclude plaiting of hair, the wearing of gold, pearls and costly raiment, and believing that a form that agrees with the spirit of the teaching is helpful in maintaining the principles of plainness and simplicity in dress and adornment in the general church body, "it seemed good to us" to submit the following restatement.
>
> 1. that the brethren wear plain clothing. That the coat with the standing collar be worn, especially by the ministers and deacons.
>
> 2. that the brethren wear their hair and beard in a plain and sanitary manner. That the mustache alone is forbidden.
>
> 3. that the sisters attire themselves in plainly-made garments, free from ornaments and unnecessary appendages. That plain bonnets and hoods be the headdress, and the hair be worn in a becoming Christian manner.
>
> 4. that the veil be worn in time of prayer and prophesying (1 Cor. 11:1-16, R.V.). The plain cap is regarded as meeting the requirements of scriptural teaching on the subject.
>
> 5. that gold for ornament, and

jewelry of all kinds, shall not be worn.

6. that no brother be installed into office as minister or deacon who will not pledge himself to observe and teach the order of dress.

7. that no brother or sister serve as delegate to District or Annual Meeting, nor be appointed on committees to enforce discipline, who does not observe the order of dress.

8. that it be the duty of the official body of the church to teach faithfully and intelligently the simple, Christian life in dress; and bishops, who are the shepherds of the churches, are required to teach and to see that the simple life in general is taught and observed in their respective charges.

9. that those who do not fully conform to the methods herein set forth, but who manifest no inclination to follow the unbecoming fashions, and whose life and conduct is becoming a follower of Christ, be dealt with in love and forbearance; and that every effort be made to save all to the church until they see the beauty of making a larger sacrifice for Christ and the church. But if, after every effort has been made, they, in an arbitrary spirit, refuse to conform to said methods, and follow the foolish fashions of the world, they may be dealt with as disorderly members; and in dealing with such cases, both the salvation of souls and the purity of the church should be kept in view.

10. that all are urged and implored, in the bonds of brotherly love and Christian fellowship, to teach and exemplify the order of the church in dress as a suitable expression of the "hidden man of the heart, in the incorruptible apparel of a meek and quiet spirit, which is in the sight of God of great price."

11. that upon the final adopting of this report it shall supersede all else in the Minutes on the subject of dress. (92:5)

Answer: Report adopted.

Section 11 had requested that a committee be appointed to do further research on the subject and provide instructional techniques and mate-

rials on the issue.

Several points should be noted regarding the report: that scriptural and historical grounds were presented for modest plain dress which differed from the world, that specific items of dress were required and prohibited, that the ministering brethren and their wives were required to wear it as exemplary members, that it was the duty of the church both to teach members and to discipline offenders, and that it superseded all previous minutes on dress. Section 9 stated the prescribed dress as the ideal, but no longer was it to be made a test of fellowship. The membership was divided into two groups: those who wore the prescribed order of dress, and those who dressed simply but not in the order, with the hope that they would soon adopt it. During this probationary period, it was the duty of the church to nurture such members for growth in spiritual matters until they saw the joy of conforming to the Gospel and thus to the order of dress. However, any member who showed no inclination toward simplicity in dress and disregarded the teachings of the church and admonishing of the presiding elder or deacons was subject to counsel by the local church. After being admonished without change in behavior, the offending member was to be disfellowshiped and lost to eternal perdition, or until such a time as he should repent and be received again into the church. Thus the church would be "purified" as the report required.

Of the many articles written about the dress decision of 1911, these brief quotations have been selected. The editor of *The Gospel Messenger* wrote regarding the report.

> The report as we view it, is a good one, and ought to be well received by all the churches. It is not as radical as some desired, nor is it as liberal as some others would have been pleased to see it, but it certainly is in keeping the judgement of the bulk of the membership of the church.
>
> One thing is certain,— it contains fully as much as may be found in the New

Testament on the dress questions. So far as a conference decision is concerned it contains a good deal more than the Church of the Brethren had for 150 years. If wisely applied, it probably contains all that may be needed to carry out the simplicity set forth in the Gospel. (110:377)

Later on that same year H.C. Early, a member of the second committee, and moderator of the Annual Meeting of 1910 and moderator-elect for 1912, wrote:

> The approximate unanimity with which the report was accepted, indicates that it expresses the mind of the Brotherhood; it indicates also that the report embraces substantially the points of value in the old Minutes, that it is a restatement in view of present needs....
>
> The adoption of the report has been followed by a peaceful, hopeful tone of feeling, widespread throughout the Brotherhood... doing away with all spirit of division since it is a compromise between radical extremes, pointing out, as it does, middle ground on which all can safely unite... (127:633)

Subsequent Action Regarding the Decision of 1911. The General Mission Board discussed the matter of teaching plain dress at its first meeting after the decision of 1911. Qualified writers were to be contacted to submit articles for publication. (140:505) This procedure was further endorsed by the Annual Meeting of 1912. The attitude taken in this instance was one of teaching rather than restraining erring members.

The unity in dress desired by the church did not increase. An attempt to tighten the rules was made by changing the wording of Article III, Section 9, at the Annual Meeting of 1915. It had read "they may be dealt with as disorderly members". It then read "they *shall* be dealt with as disorderly members". (73:154+) Other queries were sent to Annual Meeting in 1912, 1913, 1915, 1916, 1917, 1919, 1921, and 1922. They lacked the support of the voting body and were "respectfully returned" to the churches from

whence they came. Thus the decision on dress by the Annual Meeting of 1911 stood without further alteration and remains in force.

Discussion of the queries which were returned included several points of view. Rewording the decision of 1911 would not change the interpretation. Members who took advantage of the wording of the report should be disciplined. (124:473) The church was becoming congregational by making decisions at local council meetings which lacked agreement with the decisions of Annual Meeting. This caused inconsistencies in disciplining cases of members wearing fashionable dress. The probationary period regarding dress could last throughout the life of a member who had no intention of adopting the order of dress. (75:77+) It was now necessary for the church to discriminate between members who wore "plain dress", "simple and modest dress", and "fashionable dress".

Two opinions were selected from the many contributions to *The Gospel Messenger* regarding the situation on dress. One author stated "that actual church practice largely precedes rather than follows conference decisions". (132:662) The second opinion was expressed by H.C. Early in 1920, and differed from that quoted for 1911.

> Conference decisions are powerless. You cannot legislate people into goodness.... Our experience in the past, while one decision after another was passed against vanity and immodesty, if it teaches anything at all, must show the fruitlessness of law. Only grace can reach the heart. The appeal must be based on conditions within. (128:50)

The decision regarding dress by the Annual Meeting of 1911 had failed to produce uniformity in dress as was hoped by those in its favor. The church did not split over the issue of dress; neither had she attained unity on the matter. This one hundred and twenty-five year period in the history of this socio-religious group exemplified the futility of legislating dress.

Since dress is considered an index to the life style of a cultural group, then changes in the dress worn by members of this socio-religious group denoted changes in its subculture. The changes in the life style of the Brethren were summed up by the editor of *The Gospel Messenger* in 1916. The dominance of the dress issue has obscured other more important issues. The motive of the church was right in trying to apply principle to practice. Maintaining a mode of dress became more difficult because the membership had rejected a life of isolation for one of interaction with persons in the larger society. This was due in part to changes in the world at large over which the Brethren had no control. However, there were changes in the church which promoted increased interaction with the larger world: the spirit of evangelism, the interest in education, the concern for spiritual growth of the laity in the local congregation, the entrance in new occupations, and a refusal to return to an isolated way of life. (167:497) Retaining the mode of dress representative of the previous life style was therefore impossible through legislation.

Committee on Dress Reform

After the decision on dress at the Annual Meeting of 1909, a proposition was presented to the Brotherhood by D.L. Miller in *The Gospel Messenger*. He proposed that all religious and social groups interested in dress reform hold "An Anti-fashion Convention" in Washington, D.C. (140:505) The church had a history of plain dress and a message for a needy world. In accepting this proposition she would not sacrifice a single Gospel principle. Another author was of the opinion that if the world shifted to the plain dress of the church, the church would then not need to be separated from the world. (146:691) Apparently the convention never materialized, but such thinking furthered the organization of a "Committee on Dress Reform" by the church.

A Committee on Dress Reform was appointed to promote the cause of plain dressing. The activities of this committee extended over a period of fifteen years until dissolved by a reorganization of administrative boards. Its efforts, without the full support of the membership, were unable to counteract the forces of change within the church reflected in dress.

Organizational Structure. A query was sent to the Annual Meeting of 1913 requesting the appointment of a committee on dress reform. The purpose of the committee as stated in the query was "to formulate plans and confer with other religious bodies in an effort to bring about greater simplicity in dress throughout the religious world". (81:5) A committee of five members, three brethren and two sisters, was appointed to study the matter. This was the first time sisters were appointed to serve on a dress committee of any kind.

The report presented to the Annual Meeting was revised and then adopted in 1914. The methods of implementing dress reform were stated as follows:

> 3. That the committee maintain an aggressive campaign of education on the subject of dress, presenting it in the aesthetic, economic, social, moral, and religious aspects. This shall be done by special lectures, sermons and teaching, wherever possible, in the churches, schools and conference of our people and others; also through publications that will grant space for the material. (82:5)

From the time of the inception of the committee in 1914 until its merger with the Welfare Board, a total of five sisters and three brethren served on the committee. By action of the Annual Meeting of 1924 the committee was merged with two other reform committees and given the title, "Welfare Board". Two sisters on this board were to direct the work of dress reform. The last report located concerning the activities of the committee was found in the

Yearbook for 1928. (151:59) The assumption has been made by the author that activities ceased in part due to a dearth of funds because of the economic crisis of the church and the nation as a whole. It has been assumed further that the members of the church as a whole were no longer supportive of a movement of this kind.

Financial Support. Funds for the work of the Committee on Dress Reform were from two sources, private contributions from individuals and local churches and the treasury of Annual Meeting. Financial reports of the committee show that disbursements were the highest for 1924, totaling $1,162.00 (88:46) as compared to $142.68 in 1919. (85:33) The work of dress reform endeavors at the local and district levels was financed by local and district funds.

Activities. Requests of the Committee on Dress Reform were granted by Annual Meeting in 1915. They proposed that one lesson on the "simple life" be included each year in the lesson outlines for Christian Worker's Meetings. A review of the program booklets from 1916 to 1924 showed that one and more often two lesson outlines were included. These outlines were prepared by members of the committee. The committee also proposed that a sermon on the simple life be preached annually in local churches. Lastly, the committee requested time on the program of Annual Meeting for a "Women's Conference" to deal with some phase of the simple life. (83:25)

Perhaps the greatest impact of the committee was made through its programs at Annual Meeting. Prominent leaders in the church were requested to speak, and members flocked to hear them. Speakers chose such titles as: "Christian Adornment" (148:409), "The Price of Fashion" (129:372), and "Maintaining the Simple Life" (160:38). Many of these speeches were printed and distributed throughout the Brotherhood. Winners of a speech contest, using similar topics

and sponsored by the commitee, presented their orations to the crowds at Annual Meeting. (160:38) Returned missionaries spoke of the customs and dress of foreign lands. (131:385) A book counter and information center provided literature for interested members. (130:389)

Field work of the members of the Committee on Dress Reform consisted of personal visitation at district meetings and local churches. Attempts were made to organize committees on dress reform at the district and local level. The success of these attempts has not been ascertained.

In cooperation with other religious and social movements pushing dress reform, a Bureau of Information was established by the Committee on Dress Reform. Its purpose was to receive and disseminate information in regard to dress. In 1918 seventy-five items of correspondence were received monthly. (159:29) The author has not become aware of the location of any of the materials submitted.

At the recommendation of the Committee on Dress Reform in 1918, two of its members attended the Biennial Convention of the General Federation of Women's Clubs. They saw modelled the "Biennial Dress" and standardized suits promoted because of war conditions. The activities of the Biennial Conventions were reflected in later programs of the Women's Conferences at Annual Meeting. (162:133)

Standardized Clothing for the Sisters. Women of the church who no longer made their own clothing found it difficult to buy acceptable items from stores stocking fashionable clothing. The promotion of standardized styles for the sisters by the Committee on Dress Reform was considered a possible means of eliminating the evils of fashion. In 1918 the committee contracted clothing manufacturers who were willing to take orders for ready-made garments. Plans failed at this time because of the scarcity of fabrics and wartime prices. (159:30)

A special catalog was offered by the committee in the spring of 1919 to sisters desirous of standardized clothing. Three styles of standardized suits were offered. The prices quoted were as low as business conditions permitted. (161:227) The author has not located the catalog mentioned, any advertisements showing the three styles of standardized suits promoted, nor a photograph of a person wearing such a suit. How extensively they were adopted by the sisters has not been determined. The assumption has been made that only a very limited number were ever purchased by the sisters. Several reasons have been surmised. Many sisters continued to make their own dresses and therefore bought coats instead of suits. Perhaps the prices were too high, for only a few sisters worked outside the home at that time. Since suits of this type were worn by persons outside the sisterhood, they did not designate the wearer as a member of the church. Lastly, sisters who had laid aside plain dress did not wish to be restricted or to adopt another "uniform".

Nothing has been found by the author regarding the promotion or purchase of a standardized dress. Sources of other clothing and accessory items were listed by the committee. The items included were prayer caps, bonnets, shirtwaists, shoes, wristwatches, and pendant watches and guards. The watches offered had silver cases in accordance with the rules of the church.

Chapter 6

SUMMARY, CONCLUSIONS, AND RECOMMENDATIONS

Summary

This study consisted of an investigation of the origin, significance, and demise of the mode of dress worn by the members of the Church of the Brethren, from its founding in 1708 in Germany to 1970 in America. Emphasis has been placed on the period during which a particular mode of dress was prescribed for membership in the church. This period extended over the nineteenth century and the early part of the twentieth century.

Aims of This Study

The five types of resources available for investigation were: books and costume collections concerning western world costume in general; books on church history, pamphlets, tracts, periodicals, minutes of business meetings, recorded addresses, and a few photographs; family records in the form of family histories, ledgers, letters, diaries, and photographs; items of clothing; and knowledgeable persons who provided information through correspondence and personal interviews. From these resources it was possible to prepare a concise record of the prescribed mode of dress worn by members of the church. This record will serve as a resource guide on costume for the church historian, dramatist, illustrator, and publisher. Hair styles and items of clothing were identified which had both religious and social significance. Changes are noted in the mode of dress prescribed and in the items of clothing worn with the passage of time. The extent of the membership wearing the prescribed mode of dress in 1970 was observed.

Prescribed Items of Clothing.

Hair styles and items of clothing which were prescribed for church membership and thus identified a brother as a member during the nineteenth century were: a full beard, with or without a mustache; a hair style which reached the collar of his white shirt; a broad-brimmed black felt hat; a cutaway frock coat with clerical collar; and the absence of a necktie and gold jewelry. Graveclothes were the same with the exception of the hat. These items were modified gradually and by 1970 included: a shorter hair style with or without a beard, a higher-crowned hat with narrow brim, and a sack coat with clerical collar, worn without a necktie.

Hair styles and items of clothing which were prescribed for church membership and thus identified a sister as a member during the nineteenth century were: long hair, fashioned into a bun; a white cap; a bonnet; a dress cape and apron worn over a one- or two-piece dress with fitted bodice, long fitted sleeves, and a long gathered skirt; a shawl; and the absence of jewelry. Graveclothes were the same with the exception of the bonnet and shawl. These items were modified gradually and by 1970 included: long hair, fashioned into a bun; a small white cap; a small bonnet; a dress cape with waistband worn over a dress with a loosely fitted bodice, three-quarter length sleeves, a shorter gored skirt; and the absence of decorative jewelry.

The situation of the church membership in 1970 regarding the wearing of the prescribed dress was analyzed as follows: a few members were wearing "plain dress", the style subsequent to the changes wrought with the passage of time; a somewhat larger group of members were subscribing to some aspect of plain dress, such as a cap for a sister and the absence of a necktie for a brother; and the majority of members were wearing no item of clothing identifying membership in the church, having adopted the fashionable attire of their socio-economic class.

Church Polity Regarding Dress.

During the nineteenth century and early part of the twentieth century, the church perceived it her duty to regulate the manner of dressing by the membership. The passage of rules had four purposes: to carry out the directives of the scriptures, to retain the purity of the church, to maintain a spirit of unity within the church, and to save individuals from eternal perdition. Rules, or sumptuary laws, regarding dress passed by the church at the local, district, and particularly at the national level were analyzed. Four types of rules were found: those opposing ostentation in dress, and thus fashionable dress; those dealing with a particular hair style or item of clothing; those listing dress requirements for membership and for holding a particular office in the church; and those giving a method for dealing with deviant members and factions at the local level. Sources of authority for prescribing a mode of dress were arranged in a hierarchy in the following descending order: the Gospels, the remainder of the New Testament, the Old Testament, the decisions of Annual Meeting, and Brethren custom.

Two reasons for divergencies from the prescribed mode of dress were given: the lack of self-denial on the part of members and the acceptance of members not reared in the Brethren tradition. Irregularities in the wearing of the prescribed mode of dress and inconsistencies in disciplining erring members caused further tightening of the rules. This increased stringency created even greater dissatisfaction causing some members to defect. As a result the issue of dress in its totality was brought before the church in 1909. The rules were changed to coincide with the practice of the membership. In 1911 the church ruled that the prescribed mode of dress was the ideal, but it was no longer to be made a test of membership. Members who dressed simply and not in fashionable dress could be retained within the fellowship, with the intent that they would adopt the prescribed mode of dress. This decision stands with only minor alterations and remains in force.

Beliefs Reflected in the Mode of Dress.

Brethren beliefs reflected in the mode of dress prescribed during the nineteenth and early part of the twentieth centuries were evident in the resource material. The prescribed mode of dress fulfilled the function of modesty and provided physical comfort. Its lack of ornamentation gave a simplicity to individual parts which blended into a harmonious ensemble, signifying an ordering of life and serenity of spirit. Ostentation in dress was considered evil because it promoted pride in personal appearance, denounced by the scripture. A distinctive dress differing from fashionable dress denoted a separation from worldliness. Since infant baptism was rejected, the prescribed mode of dress was not adopted by an individual until baptized, usually as a young adult. Since equality in rank was held as an ideal, clothing did not differ between officiant and lay members of the group. However, the two sexes were not equated and transvestitism was unacceptable. The broad-brimmed black hat was adopted by the brethren and the mustache was rejected when worn alone because of pacifistic views. The clerical collar for the brethren and the cap for the sisters were interpreted as signifying the priesthood of each believer.

The Brethren believed that the Bible required the wearing of certain hair styles and items of clothing and the abstaining from wearing others. Plain dress promoted spirituality in the wearer. The way of the Brethren was "right". The founding Brethren were exemplary and deviation from their manner of dressing was "wrong". The purifying of the church was the duty of the governing bodies. Methods included the passing of rules, or sumptuary laws, to control the manner of dressing; and by the use of such disciplinary measures as admonishment, avoidance, and excommunication. Individuals whose beliefs differed from those of the Brethren were viewed as condemned to eternal perdition.

After 1900 the views of the Brethren were closer to those of a church rather than a sect. These enlarged views of the Brethren were reflected in their mode of dress. The New Testament demanded simplicity and modesty in dress, but not conformity to a particular mode. Concern for spiritual matters took precedence over the dressing of the physical body. Propriety in dress was a personal matter, but was not to be overlooked by exemplary Christians. The duty of the church was to nurture deviant members, rather than excommunicate them. The mode of dress was to promote rather than impede evangelizing the world. Force was being used in religion when the church prescribed a mode of dress.

Conclusions

The mode of dress worn by the members of the Church of the Brethren was a unique product of their religious beliefs and cultural setting in America during the nineteenth century. It represented a people living on the frontier, seeking a livelihood from the soil, and isolated from the luxury of imports and the influence of fashionable dress. A period of time was required to synthesize a mode of dress which identified the wearer as a member of this socio-religious group. The distinctiveness of the dress was dependent upon the extent of the interaction by group members with the larger society. The mode of dress became a visible symbol of the religious beliefs held by the group, or rejected by it. As the life style of the Brethren became an ideal, this particular mode of dress was considered as ideal. Once the mode of dress was synthesized, there were objections to changes in the items or exchanges for other items.

With the acceleration of change in fashionable dress the difference between it and Brethren dress became more noticeable, despite minor changes in the latter. The frugality of the Brethren in this setting did not permit frequent changes in clothing styles, or the disposal of garments which were not worn out. However the presence of some elements of fashionable dress did appear in the plain dress, and made it possible to date items.

Only a minimal number of items of outer wear were necessary to designate an individual as holding membership in this subculture group. Hierarchies of adoption and demise of clothing items were noted in regard to age, status, occasion and locale of a member. More elderly members than young members wore prescribed items. More officiary members than lay members wore prescribed items. If a cap was worn daily by a sister, it was worn for all religious services. If not worn daily and if worn at all it was worn for the most sacred occasion, the communion service. During their life span, some members changed the number and type of prescribed items they wore. In making the change from plain to fashionable dress, items signifying the latter status were adopted gradually. The last item of plain dress laid aside by a sister was her cap. The last item of fashionable dress adopted by a brother was a necktie. The prescribed items were laid aside earlier in the twentieth century by members residing in the western part of the Brotherhood, than in the more densely populated areas in the eastern part.

The prescribed items of clothing were not static but reflected changes in regard to season, occasion, locale, and period of time. The prescribed items of clothing worn by the sisters which reflected seasonal changes were their bonnets, dresses, and shawls. Items of clothing worn by the brethren which reflected a difference between Sunday and daily wear were their coats, shirts, and hats. Slight differences in cut and detail were noted particularly in the caps and bonnets worn in various locales throughout the Brotherhood. With the passage of time the greatest change was noted in the headdress worn by the sisters. The large cap and bonnet worn in the nineteenth century was gradually reduced in size until only a portion of the crown of each remained in 1970. The clerical collar was retained on the coat of the brethren, but the remainder was subject to changes observed in fashionable coats. As changes were made in the prescribed items, they were accepted as meeting the requirements and considered to be "correct". When items of the prescribed clothing were not worn continually, a means of storage was worked out in each instance. The color of the prescribed items did not appear as an issue in the discussions and rulings concerning dress. Items of clothing not prescribed were selected in colors and textures to harmonize with those prescribed. As technological developments brought new fibers into fabrics, selections were made in keeping with plain dress.

Securing the necessary clothing items prescribed for membership required expenditure of the private purse. The frugality of the Brethren permitted them to change from the lower to the middle socio-economic class. With an increase in discretionary spending, a portion was spent on clothing, indicative of this new status. The temptations offered by an industrialized garment industry were not always resisted. The "simplicity" of Brethren dress was questioned when garment styles of fashionable clothing became simpler in cut and detail and when they cost less than the prescribed items.

The individual items of clothing adopted by the Brethren had both historical precedent and symbolic meaning. The headdress was the most significant. The two most contested items and the last two to be ruled upon by the authoritative body were the beards of the brethren and the caps of the sisters. With passage of time the symbolic meaning of these two items and other items changed. The cap as a requisite for worship retained significance after it was discarded as a symbol of marriage. The higher-crowned hat worn by the brethren at the end of the nineteenth century no longer inferred the wearer as holding pacifistic beliefs. The custom of wearing wedding rings is no longer considered sinful by a majority of the members, although the wearing of gold is ruled out by the scripture.

The Brethren were sincere in their attempts to control dress as a means of promoting proper conduct on the part of each member. The affirmation of faith was expanded to include a promise to conform to the order of dress. The new member was allowed a probationary period in which to adopt the prescribed items, but he was not to take advantage of the situation. Greater adherence in both precept and example was expected of an officiant. The only reasons for excusing a member were for those of health. A change from the prescribed mode of dress denoted a departure from the ways of the Brethren. The witness to beliefs was to be consistent regardless of the occasion, religious or social, and regardless of the locale, among the Brethren or outsiders. Outsiders were not always aware of doctrinal statements and scriptural proofs, but they had an inkling whether the manner of living was consistent with a member's dress. They were perceptive to changes and were quick to observe inconsistencies from their point of view.

A prerequisite for prescribing a mode of dress was the development of a church government with authority and strength adequate for its enforcement. The rules passed by Annual Meeting concerning non-conformity to the world in regard to the manner of dressing by the membership were found to be consistent. Early decisions of a general nature were made more specific because of test cases. Once this trend was started, it accelerated until no further rules were considered necessary, only adherence to those already on the minutes.

Although widespread, complete conformity to a mode of dress was never achieved. The issue of clothing increased in intensity during the major schisms in the church and during the desire for unity in thought on the matter. Because of inconsistencies between the rules and practice by the membership, the issue in its totality was opened for reconsideration. The rules were changed in an effort to make practice coincide with the decisions of the authoritative body, although some members considered the decision of 1911 to be a compromise.

Without the support of the membership, the rules and efforts of a committee on dress reform were inadequate to withstand the forces of change operating upon the subculture of the group, and therefore upon the mode of dress worn by the Brethren. No evidence of a trend toward the adoption of a new mode of dress distinctive to the membership was observed during this study. The mode of dress worn in the nineteenth century will not reappear because, in all probability, the distinctive cultural setting and particular beliefs which spawned it will not return.

Recommendations

Of further interest beyond the scope of this study are: the adaptations made in the prescribed dress by Church of the Brethren missionaries on foreign fields of service and how converts responded; the mode of dress worn by the Old German Baptist Brethren and the Dunkard Brethren, deleted from this study; changes in prescribed attire resulting from an increase in discretionary funds; the impact of internal and external interaction on the clothing prescribed for membership in subcultural groups; and the mental health of individuals who conform or deviate from a mode of dress prescribed by a socio-religious group.

BIBLIOGRAPHY and SOURCES

Books

1. "Apron." *Oxford English Dictionary*, 1961. Vol. 1.

2. Bittinger, Desmond W. "And How Shall The Brethren Be Recognized?" *The Adventurous Future: A Compilation of Addresses, Papers, Statements, and Messages Associated with the Celebration of the Two Hundred-fiftieth Anniversary of the Church of the Brethren*. An Anniversary Volume, 1708-1958. Comp. and ed. by Paul H. Bowman. Elgin, Illinois: The Brethren Press, 1959.

3. Bittinger, Emmert F. *Heritage and Promise: Perspectives on the Church of the Brethren*. Elgin, Illinois: The Brethren Press, 1970.

4. Brumbaugh, Martin G. *A History of the German Baptist Brethren in Europe and America*. Mount Morris, Illinois: Brethren Publishing House, 1899.

5. *Chronicon Ephratense; A History of the Community of Seventh Day Baptists at Ephrata, Lancaster County, Pennsylvania*, by "Lamech" and "Agrippa". Translated from the original German by J.M. Hark. Lancaster, Pennsylvania: S.H. Zahn and Co., 1889.

6. Church of the Brethren. *History of the Church of the Brethren of the Eastern District of Pennsylvania*. By the committee appointed by District Conference. Lancaster, Pennsylvania: The New Era Printing Company, 1915.

7. Cohen, Albert. "Deviant Behavior." *International Encyclopedia of the Social Sciences*, 1968. Vol. 4.

8. "Costume, Ecclesiastical." *Encyclopedia Americana*, 1970. Vol. 8.

9. Cunnington, Phyllis. *Costume in Pictures, A Dutton Vista Picturebook*. London: Studio Vista Limited, 1964.

10. Deutsch, Morton. "Groups: Group Behavior." *International Encyclopedia of the Social Sciences*, 1968. Vol. 6.

11. Durandus, William. *The Symbolism of Churches and Church Ornaments*. London: Gibbings and Company, Ltd., 1893.

12. Durnbaugh, Donald F. *The Brethren in Colonial America. A Source Book on the Transplantation and Development of the Church of the Brethren in the Eighteenth Century*. Elgin, Illinois: The Brethren Press, 1967.

13. _____. *European Origins of the Brethren; A Source Book on the Beginnings of the Church of the Brethren in the Early Eighteenth Century*. Elgin, Illinois: The Brethren Press, 1958.

14. Earle, Alice M. *Costume of Colonial Times*. New York: Charles Scribner's Sons, 1917.

15. Emmert, David. *Reminiscences of Juniata College, 1876-1901.* Illustrated and published by the author, Huntingdon, Pennsylvania, 1901.

16. Falkenstein, George N. *History of the German Baptist Brethren Church.* Lancaster, Pennsylvania: The New Era Printing Company, 1901.

17. Fausset, Andrew R. *Bible Encycolpedia and Dictionary, Critical and Expository.* Grand Rapids, Michigan: Zondervan Publishing House, n.d.

18. Fletcher, Stevenson W. *Pennsylvania Agriculture and Country Life, 1640-1840.* Harrisburg: Pennsylvania Historical and Museum Commission, 1950.

19. Gillin, John L. "Dunkers". *The New Schaff-Herzog Encyclopedia of Religious Knowledge*, 1959. Vol. 4.

20. Graeff, Arthur D. "Pennsylvania, The Colonial Melting Pot". *The Pennsylvania Germans,* ed. Ralph Wood. Princeton, New Jersey: Princeton University Press, 1942.

21. Hazeltine, H.D. "Excommunication." *Encyclopedia of the Social Sciences,* 1937. Vol. 5.

22. Helman, Cora W. *A Heap of Living.* Stories Concerning the J. Edson Ulreys and the Church of the Brethren at Onekama, Michigan, no imprint.

23. Helman, Harley H. *Church of the Brethren in Southern Ohio.* Compiled by the Historical Committee, authorized by the District of Southern Ohio. Elgin, Illinois: Brethren Publishing House, 1955.

24. Hoebel, E. Adamson. *Man in the Primitive World. An Introduction to Anthropology.* 2d. ed. New York: McGraw Hill Book Co., 1958.

25. Honigmann, John J. *The World of Man.* New York: Harper and Brothers, 1959.

26. Horn, Marilyn J. *The Second Skin, An Interdisciplinary Study of Clothing.* Boston: Houghton Mifflin Co., 1968.

27. Howe, Roland L. *The History of a Church (Dunker) with Comments Featuring the First Church of the Brethren of Philadelphia, Pa., 1813-1943.* Lancaster, Pennsylvania: Lancaster Press, Inc., 1943.

28. Hyman, Herbert H. "Reference Groups". *International Encyclopedia of the Social Sciences,* 1968. Vol. 13.

29. Kessing, Felix M. *Cultural Anthropology, The Science of Culture.* New York: Rinehart and Co., 1958.

30. "Kerchief." *Oxford English Dictionary*, 1961. Vol. 5.

31. Keyser, Naaman H., *et al. History of Old Germantown with a Description of Its Settlement and Some Account of Its Important Persons, Buildings, and Places Connected With Its Development.* Germantown, Philadelphia: H.F. McCann, publisher, 1907.

32. Kollmorgan, Walter M. "The Pennsylvania German Farmer". *The Pennsylvania Germans,* ed. Ralph Wood. Princeton, New Jersey: Princeton University Press, 1942.

33. Laver, James. *The Concise History of Costume and Fashion.* New York: Harry

N. Abrams, Inc., n.d.

34. Mallott, Floyd E. *Studies in Brethren History*. Elgin, Illinois: Brethren Publishing House, 1954.

35. Miller, John E. *The Story of Our Church for Young People of the Church of the Brethren*. Elgin Illinois: Brethren Publishing House, 1941.

36. Moore, J.H. "Dunkers." *The New Schaff-Herzog Encyclopedia of Religious Knowledge*, 1959. Vol. 4.

37. Nead, Peter. *Theological Writings on Various Subjects; or a Vindication of Primitive Christianity as Recorded in the Word of God*. Published for the author by B.F. Ellis, Dayton, Ohio, 1850.

38. Neher, Medford D. *A Mural History of the Church of the Brethren in Twelve Panels Painted by Medford D. Neher*. Account by L.W. Shultz. Milford, Indiana, 1953.

39. Niebuhr, H. Richard. "Sects." *Encyclopedia of the Social Sciences*, 1937. Vol. 13.

40. O'Dea, Thomas F. "Sects and Cults." *International Encyclopedia of the Social Sciences*, 1968. Vol. 14.

41. "Pride." *Oxford English Dictionary*. 1968. Vol. 8.

42. Rose, Arnold M. (ed.) *Human Behavior and Social Processes*. Boston: Houghton Mifflin Co., 1962.

43. Royer, Galen B. "The Development of Missions in the Church." *Two Centuries of the Church of the Brethren*. Bicen-

tennial Addresses at the Annual Conference, Held at Des Moines, Iowa, June 3-11, 1908. Elgin, Illinois: Brethren Publishing House, 1908.

44. Sack, Saul. *History of Higher Education in Pennsylvania*. Harrisburg: The Pennsylvania Historical and Museum Commission, 1963.

45. Sappington, Roger E. *Brethren Social Policy, 1908-1958*. Elgin, Illinois: The Brethren Press, 1961.

46. Senger, Nettie M. *"House of Sanger", History of the Descendents of Conrad Sanger, Son of John Senger*. Nashville, Tennessee: Ambrose Printing Co., 1956.

47. Sherif, Muzafer and Carolyn W. Sherif. *Reference Groups: Exploration into Conformity and Deviation of Adolescents*. New York: Harper and Row, Publishers, 1964.

48. Shibutani, Tamotsu. "Reference Groups and Social Control". ed. Arnold M. Rose. *Human Behavior and Social Processes*. Boston: Houghton Mifflin Co., 1962.

49. "Shoe." *The World Book Encyclopedia*, 1956. Vol. 15.

50. Shultz. Lawrence W. *Schwarzenau, Yesterday and Today*. Published by the author at Milford, Indiana, 1954.

51. Stone, Gregory P. "Appearance and the Self." *Human Behavior and Social Processes*. ed. A. M. Rose. Boston: Houghton Mifflin Co., 1962.

52. Swanson, Guy E. "Interaction: Symbolic Interaction." *International Encyclopedia of the Social Sciences*, 1968. Vol. 7.

53. Vincent, J.M. "Sumptuary Legislation." *Encyclopedia of the Social Sciences*, 1937. Vol. 14.

54. Warwick, Edward, Henry C. Pitz, and Alexander Wyckoff. *Early American Dress, The Colonial and Revolutionary Periods*. Vol. 2. New York: Benjamin Blom, 1965.

55. *Webster's New World Dictionary*. College ed. Cleveland: The World Publishing Co., 1968.

56. Weddle, Ethel H. *Pleasant Hill*. Elgin, Illinois: Brethren Publishing House, 1956.

57. Wood, Julia. *Closed Communion*. Huntingdon, Pennsylvania: Pilgrim's Office, 1875.

58. Zelditch, Morris, Jr. "Status, Social." *International Encyclopedia of the Social Sciences*, 1968. Vol. 15.

Minutes

59. Church of the Brethren. *Classified Minutes of the Annual Meetings of the Church of the Brethren: A History of the General Councils of the Church from 1778 to 1885*. Mount Morris, Illinois, and Huntingdon, Pennsylvania: The Brethren Publishing Company, 1886.

60. Church of the Brethren. *Full Report of the Proceedings of the Annual Meeting of the Church of the Brethren*. Huntingdon, Pennsylvania: Quinter and Brumbaugh Bros., 1876. Later editions by various publishers.

61. _____. 1877.

62. _____. 1881.

63. _____. 1886.

64. _____. 1889.

65. _____. 1893.

66. _____. 1898.

67. _____. 1899.

68. _____. 1900.

69. _____. 1909.

70. _____. 1910.

71. _____. 1911.

72. _____. 1912.

73. _____. 1915.

74. _____. 1918.

75. _____. 1922.

76. _____. 1925.

77. _____. 1926.

78. Church of the Brethren. *Minutes of the Annual Conferences of the Church of the Brethren, 1923-1944*. Compiled and edited by H.L. Hartsough, J.E. Miller, and Ora W. Garber. Elgin, Illinois: Brethren Publishing House, 1946.

79. Church of the Brethren. *Minutes of the Annual Meeting of the Church of the Brethren*. Elgin, Illinois: Brethren Publishing House, 1910.

80. _____. 1911.

81. _____. 1913.

82. _____. 1914.

83. _____. 1915.

84. _____. 1918.

85. _____. 1919.

86. _____. 1920.

87. _____. 1923.

88. _____. 1924.

89. _____. 1925.

90. Church of the Brethren. *Minutes of the Annual Meetings of the Brethren.* Dayton, Ohio: Christian Publishing Association, 1876.

91. Church of the Brethren. *Minutes of the Annual Meetings of the Church of the Brethren Containing All Available Minutes from 1778-1909.* Elgin, Illinois: Brethren Publishing House, 1909.

92. Church of the Brethren. *Revised Minutes of the Annual Meetings of the Church of the Brethren from 1778 to 1922.* Revised by Otho Winger, J.H. Longenecker, and George L. Studebaker, Committee Appointed by the Annual Conference of 1917. Elgin, Illinois: Brethren Publishing House, 1922.

93. Church of the Brethren. Districts. Eastern Pennsylvania. *Minutes of District Meeting.* 1897-1944. Place of publication varies.

94. Church of the Brethren. Districts. Eastern Pennsylvania. *Minutes of the District Meetings of the German Baptist Brethren of the Eastern District of Pennsylvania.* 1867 to 1896. Lansdale, Pennsylvania: Press of Lansdale "Republican".

95. Church of the Brethren. Districts. Eastern Pennsylvania. *Minutes of the Elders in Session at District Meeting.* 1897-1918. Place of publication varies.

96. Church of the Brethren. Districts. Southern Pennsylvania. *Minutes of the District Conference.* 1920-1944. Published by the District, various places.

97. Church of the Brethren. Spring Creek Congregation. "Minutes of the Council Meetings". 1879 to 1921. Manuscript copy in the library of Frank S. Carper, Palmyra, Pennsylvania.

Pamphlets, Tracts, and Leaflets

98. *The Brethren's Card.* Elgin, Illinois: Brethren Publishing House, 1923.

99. Doll, Eugene E. *The Ephrata Cloister, An Introduction.* Ephrata, Pennsylvania: The Ephrata Cloister Associates, 1958.

100. *History of the Mexico Church of the Brethren, Indiana, Centennial Program.* 1941.

101. Mack, Alexander. *A Plain View of the Rites and Ordinances of the House of God, Arranged in the Form of a Conversation Between Father and Son; to Which Are Added Ground Searching*

Questions, Answered by the Author, 1715. A translation printed by The Brethren's Publishing Company, Mount Morris, Illinois, 1888.

102. Newcomer, H.E. "To the Ministers of the Brethren Church." Mount Morris, Illinois: July 1890. Copy available at Beeghley Library, Juniata College, Huntingdon, Pennsylvania.

103. Pentz, Dorothy S. *Our Living Church: Coventry Church of the Brethren.* Pottstown, Pennsylvania: Mahr Printing, Inc., 1963.

Periodicals

104. Advertisement: Albaugh Bros., Dover Co. *The Inglenook*, Vol. 8, August 21, 1906, p. 818.

105. Advertisement: The Brethren Publishing House. *The Gospel Messenger*, Vol. 66, September 1, 1917, p. 559.

106. Advertisement: H. E. Newcomer. *The Gospel Messenger*, Vol. 36, July 2, 1898, p. 416.

107. Advertisement: Larimer Manufacturing Co. *Brethren Family Almanac*, 1903, p. 2.

108. Advertisement: Mary Brubaker. *Brethren Family Almanac*, 1902, p. 54.

109. "Annual Meeting Notes." *The Gospel Messenger*, Vol. 49, June 18, 1910, p. 393.

110. "Annual Meeting Notes." *The Gospel*

Messenger, Vol. 50, June 7, 1911, p. 377.

111. "Annual Meeting Notes." *The Gospel Messenger*, Vol. 51, June 15, 1912, p. 380.

112. "Annual Meeting Queries." *The Gospel Messenger*, Vol. 42, January 31, 1903, p. 74.

113. "Annual Meeting Queries." *The Gospel Messenger*, Vol. 49, April 30, 1910, p. 286.

114. "Back to I Cor. 11." *The Gospel Messenger,* Vol. 46, June 6, 1908, p. 362.

115. Balsbaugh, C.H. "Must It Be." *The Gospel Messenger*, Vol. 25, June 21, 1887, p. 370.

116. Beery, Charles O. "Sunday-School Pins and Buttons." *The Gospel Messenger*, Vol. 51, October 12, 1912, p. 643.

117. Bright, John Calvin. "History of the Brethren in Southern Ohio for a Century." *Brethren Family Almanac*, 1906, p. 29.

118. Brown, Dale W. "The Dunker Costume and the Mod Generation." *Messenger*, Vol. 120, April 15, 1971, pp. 20-22.

119. _____. "Membership in the Body of Christ as Interpreted by the Heritage of the Brethren." *Brethren Life and Thought*, Vol. 9, Autumn 1964, pp. 63-64.

120. Brumbaugh, H.B. "The Dress Problem." *The Gospel Messenger*, Vol. 33, March 26, 1895, p. 201.

121. "Building a Church." *The Youngstown Vindicator*, Rotogravure Section. January 24, 1971.

122. Cassel, Abraham. "On Feet-Washing." *Christian Family Companion*, Vol. 8, April 1872, pp. 230-31.

123. *Christian Worker's Meeting: Outlines of Topics*. 1909 to 1934. Brethren Publishing House, Elgin, Illinois.

124. "The Dress Question Settled." *The Gospel Messenger*, Vol. 54, July 24, 1915, pp. 473-74.

125. "During Prayer." *The Gospel Messenger*, Vol. 44, September 23, 1905, p. 601.

126. Durnbaugh, Donald F. "The Lesson in History." *Brethren Adult Quarterly*, Vol. 73, April to June, 1958.

127. Early, H.C. "The Action of the Late Conference on the Dress Question." *The Gospel Messenger*, Vol. 50, October 7, 1911, p. 633.

128. _____. "Foolish Dressing–The Remedy." *The Gospel Messenger*, Vol. 69, January 24, 1920, p. 50.

129. "Echoes from the Annual Conference." *The Gospel Messenger*, Vol. 65, June 17, 1916, p. 372.

130. "Echoes from the Calgary Conference." *The Gospel Messenger*, Vol. 72, June 23, 1923, p. 389.

131. "Echoes from the Hershey Conference." *The Gospel Messenger*, Vol. 73, June 21, 1924, p. 385.

132. Frantz, Ira H. "Decisions and Church Practice." *The Gospel Messenger*, Vol. 68, October 18, 1919, p. 662.

133. Hays, Daniel. "Annual Meeting on Dress." *The Gospel Messenger*, Vol. 48, December 25, 1909, p. 821.

134. Howard, Clifford. "A Peace Loving People." *The Ladies Home Journal*, Vol. 15, July 1898, pp. 5-6.

135. "Imposter." *The Gospel Messenger*, Vol. 27, September 10, 1889, p. 574.

136. Lloyd, Nelson. "Among the Dunkers." *Scribner's Magazine*, Vol. 30, November, 1901.

137. "Local Church Directory and Statistics for the Year Ended September 30, 1969." *Yearbook*, 1970. Published by the General Board, Church of the Brethren General Offices, Elgin, Illinois.

138. Mallott, Floyd E. "The Lesson in History." *Brethren Adult Quarterly*, Vol. 73, April to June, 1958.

139. Manchester College. *The Aurora*. Published by the Junior Class of Manchester College, North Manchester, Indiana. 1910. n.p.

140. Miller, D.L. "Teaching on Plain Dress, and the Simple Life." *The Gospel Messenger*, Vol. 51, August 10, 1912, p. 505.

141. _____. "The Unity of the Church of the Brethren." *The Gospel Messenger*, Vol. 48, May 15, 1909, p. 313.

142. Miller, J.H. "Newspaper Extract." *The Brethren's Almanac*, 1871, p. 17.

143. _____. "Pride." *The Gospel Messenger*, Vol. 25, June 21, 1887, p. 372.

144. Miller, P.S. "Concerning Credential Commitee Work." *The Gospel Messenger*, Vol. 67, July 27, 1918, p. 471.

145. Morgan, R.K. "I Took My Robe Off." *Messenger*, Vol. 177, June 6, 1968, p. 11.

146. Moyer, Elgin S. "The Responsibility of a Plain People." *The Gospel Messenger*, Vol. 65, October 28, 1916, pp. 691-92.

147. "Must the Prayer Covering Go?" *The Gospel Messenger*, Vol. 49, February 19, 1910, p. 122.

148. "Our Annual Conference Notes." *The Gospel Messenger*, Vol. 63, June 27, 1914, p. 409.

149. "Our Late District Meeting." *The Gospel Messenger*, Vol. 64, September 4, 1915, p. 569.

150. Pyle, Howard. "A Peculiar People." *Harper's New Monthly Magazine*, Vol. 79, October 1889, pp. 776-85.

151. "Report of Welfare Department." *Yearbook*, 1928, p. 59.

152. Sell, J.A., W.S. Long, and J.B. Brumbaugh. "A Meeting of Elders." *The Gospel Messenger*, Vol. 48, February 13, 1909, p. 100.

153. Sharp, S.Z. "The Token of Authority." *The Gospel Messenger*, Vol. 34, March 28, 1896, pp. 194-95.

154. Smith, John. "Elder Peter Nead." *Brethren Family Almanac*, 1909, pp. 27-31.

155. Smith, Leander. "The Bible Teaching on Dress." *The Gospel Messenger*, Vol. 50, June 17, 1911, p. 379.

156. Stamm, Hattie E. "Pride–What It Is." *The Gospel Messenger*, Vol. 48, January 16, 1909, pp. 35-36.

157. Stover, J. Harmon. "Properly Qualified Delegates." *The Gospel Messenger*, Vol. 68, October 4, 1919, pp. 626-27.

158. Swartz, F.W. "Why I Wear A Robe." *Messenger*, Vol. 118, July 31, 1969, pp, 26-27.

159. Taylor, Lydia E. "Dress Reform." *Yearbook*, 1919, p. 30.

160. _____. "Dress Reform." *Yearbook*, 1922, p. 38.

161. _____. "Standardization." *The Gospel Messenger*, Vol. 68, May 3, 1919, p. 227.

162. _____. "That Biennial Convention." *The Gospel Messenger*, Vol. 68, March 1, 1919, p. 133.

163. Teague, Flora E. "More Questions and Answers–The Prayer Covering." *The Gospel Messenger*, Vol. 40, August 2, 1902, p. 490.

164. Teeter, Lewis W. "The Devotional Covering." *The Gospel Messenger,* Vol. 50, November 4, 1911, p. 697.

165. Teeter, Mary E. "Why I Wear A Bonnet." *The Gospel Messenger*, Vol. 51, October 9, 1912, p. 710.

166. "Watch the Trunks." *The Gospel Messenger*, Vol. 33, August 22, 1893, p. 520.

167. "Where Withal Shall We Be Clothed." Part I. *The Gospel Messenger*, Vol. 65, August 5, 1916, pp. 497-98.

168. Zigler, M.R. "Elder John Kline–Churchman." *Brethren Life and Thought*, Vol. 9, Summer 1964, p.16.

Unpublished Works

169. Johnson, Mary A. "Diary". Teegarden, Marshall County, Indiana. Property of Alma Van Winkle, North Manchester, Indiana. December 22, 1885.

170. _____. July 27, 1886.

171. _____. February 1, 1887.

172. _____. March 14, 1901.

173. Miller D.L. "Prayer Veil". Sermon at Mount Morris College, Mount Morris, Illinois, March 22, 1908. Copy available at Brethren Historical Library, Elgin, Illinois.

174. Willoughby, William G. "The Beliefs of the Early Brethren." Unpublished Ph.D. dissertation, Boston University Graduate School, 1951.

Personal Letters

Personal letters to Abraham Cassel, Harleysville, Pennsylvania, are located at Beeghley Library, Juniata College, Huntingdon, Pennsylvania.

175. Auge, M. Norristown, Pennsylvania, n.d.

176. _____. March 14, 1884.

177. Bolin, Delia. Niles, Michigan, August 27, 1876.

178. Cassel, H.C. Philadelphia, Pennsylvania, November 16, 1884.

179. Frick, A.K. Philadelphia, Pennsylvania, September 20, 1869.

180. Price, C.P. Aukeneytown, Knox County, Ohio, August 28, 1880.

Personal letters to the author during the research period.

181. Durnbaugh, Donald F. Oak Brook, Illinois, May 6, 1969.

182. Gibble, Anna Ober. Manheim, Pennsylvania, September 25, 1969.

183. Holsopple, Kathren Royer. LaVerne, California, June 18, 1969.

184. Longenecker, Barbara. Neffsville, Pennsylvania, October 11, 1969.

185. Michael, Marianne K. Iowa City, Iowa, July 20, 1969.

186. Name withheld.

Personal Interviews by the Author

187. Brumbaugh, Diane. Huntingdon, Pennsylvania, July 27, 1968.

188. Carper, Ella. Palmyra, Pennsylvania, August 17, 1968.

189. Carper, Frank S. Palmyra, Pennsylvania, August 17, 1968.

190. Keeney, Anna Bashor. Bethel, Pennsylvania, August 4, 1970.

191. Laher, Ruth. Everett. Pennsylvania, August 6, 1968.

192. Martin, Harold. Elizabethtown, Pennsylvania, August 8, 1968.

193. Meyer, E.G. Elizabethtown, Pennsylvania, August 15, 1968.

194. Meyer, Mildred. New Holland, Pennsylvania, June 26, 1969

195. Pepple, D.I. Woodbury, Pennsylvania, August 5, 1968.

196. Pepple, Mary Ritchey. Woodbury, Pennsylvania, August 5, 1968.

197. Ritchey, Dessie. Saxton, Pennsylvania, July 21, 1968.

198. Rupel, Edith Rohrer. West Layfayette, Indiana, January 28, 1970.

199. _____. May 10, 1970.

200. _____. August 17, 1970.

201. Schlosser, Ralph W. Elizabethtown, Pennsylvania, August 16, 1968.

202. Taylor, Barnard C. Huntingdon, Pennsylvania, July 7, 1968.

203. Van Winkle, Alma. North Manchester, Indiana, April 2, 1970.

204. Weddle, Ethel Harshbarger. Girard, Illinois, June 27, 1969.

205. Wyles, Olyve. Martinsburg, Pennsylvania, August 5, 1968.

206. Name withheld.

Personal Visits by the Investigator

207. Annual Conference of the Church of the Brethren, Louisville, Kentucky, June 24 to 29, 1969.

208. Elizabethtown Church of the Brethren, Elizabethtown, Pennsylvania, August 11, 1968.

209. Ephrata Cloister, Ephrata, Pennsylvania, August 20, 1968.

210. First Church of the Brethren, Philadelphia, Pennsylvania, August 24, 1968.

211. Gohn Brothers Manufacturing Company and Store, Middlebury, Indiana, May 16, 1968.

212. Golden Valley Community Church, Golden Valley, Minnesota, June 20, 1967.

213. Hager's Store, Lancaster, Pennsylvania, August 16, 1968.

214. Highland Avenue Church of the Brethren, Elgin, Illinois, August 6, 1967.

215. Kokomo Church of the Brethren, Kokomo, Indiana, March 15, 1969.

216. Lafayette Church of the Brethren, Lafayette, Indiana, 1956 to 1971.

217. Manchester Church of the Brethren, North Manchester, Indiana, March 31, 1970.

218. Martin's Store, Elizabethtown, Pennsylvania, August 8, 1968.

219. Marian and Ruth Shop, Mount Joy, Pennsylvania, August 10, 1968.

220. Nettle Creek Church of the Brethren, Hagerstown, Indiana, September 4 and 5, 1970.

221. Pine Creek Church of the Brethren, North Liberty, Indiana, October 19, 1968.

222. Prince of Peace Church of the Brethren, South Bend, Indiana, October 18, 1970.

223. Rossville Church of the Brethren, Rossville, Indiana, April 17, 1968.

224. Springfield Church of the Brethren, Springfield, Oregon, December 24, 1966.

225. Stone Church of the Brethren, Huntingdon, Pennsylvania, July 7, 1968.

226. Stonerstown Church of the Brethren, Saxton, Pennsylvania, July 21, 1968.

227. White Oak Congregation, Manheim and Graybill Houses, Manheim, Pennsylvania, August 18, 1968.

228. Zion Hill Church of the Brethren, Columbiana, Ohio, September 2, 1968.

APPENDICES

APPENDIX A
Sources of Figures

1. Information gleaned from various sources on Brethren history.

2. Adapted from *Brethren Adult Quarterly*, Vol. 73, No. 2, April to June, 1958, p. 128.

3. Information from: Miller, J.E. *The Story of Our Church*. Elgin, Illinois: Brethren Publishing House, 1944.

4. Ibid.

5. "Local Church Directory and Statistics for the Year Ended September 30, 1969." *Yearbook*. Published by the General Board, Church of the Brethren General Offices, Elgin, Illinois, 1970. pp. 33-141.

6. Neher, Medford D. and Lawrence W. Schultz. *A Mural History of the Church of the Brethren*. Published by Camp Alexander Mack, Milford, Indiana. Panels I and II. pp. 6 and 8.

7. Photo loaned by the artist, Barnard C. Taylor, Huntingdon, Pennsylvania.

8. Howe, Roland L. *The History of a Church (Dunker) with Comments Featuring the First Church of the Brethren of Philadelphia, Pa. 1813-1943*. Lancaster, Pennsylvania: Lancaster Press, Inc., 1943. Frontispiece.

9. Ibid.

10. Property of First Church of the Brethren, Philadelphia, Pennsylvania.

11. Ibid.

12. Photo loaned by Donald F. Durnbaugh, Bethany Theological Seminary, Oak Brook, Illinois.

13. Doll, Eugene E. *The Ephrata Cloister*. Ephrata, Pennsylvania: The Ephrata Cloister Associates, 1958, p. 4.

14. Ibid, p. 5.

15. Ibid, cover.

16. Photo by Don Honick, Church of the Brethren General Offices, Elgin, Illinois.

17. Pentz, Dorothy Saylor. *Our Living Church: Coventry Church of the Brethren*. Pottstown, Pennsylvania: Mahr Printing, Inc., 1963, p. 5.

18. Nead, Peter. *Theological Writings on Various Subjects; or a Vindication of Primitive Christianity as Recorded in the Word of God*. Published for the author by B.F. Ellis, Dayton, Ohio, 1850, p. 72.

19. Photo loaned by Esther Austin,

Bloomington, Indiana.

20. Photo loaned by Goldie Hoover Hoel, Hagerstown, Indiana.

21. Photo loaned by Kathren Royer Holsopple, LaVerne, California.

22. Ibid.

23. Ibid.

24. Photo loaned by Juniata College, Huntingdon, Pennsylvania.

25. Photo loaned by Kathren Royer Holsopple, LaVerne, California.

26. Photo loaned by Mary Kay Rinehart, Hagerstown, Indiana.

27. Photo from the family collection of the author.

28. Manchester College: *The Aurora*. Published by the Junior Class of Manchester College. North Manchester, Indiana, 1910, n.p.

29. Photo loaned by George Hildreth, Lafayette, Indiana.

30. Photo loaned by the Brethren Historical Library, Church of the Brethren General Offices, Elgin, Illinois.

31. Property of the family of the author.

32. Photo loaned by Esther Heisler, Freeport, Michigan.

33. Photo by Don Honick, Church of the Brethren General Offices, Elgin, Illinois.

34. Nead. *Theological Writings*. p. 160.

35. Lloyd, Nelson. "Among the Dunkers." *Scribner's Magazine,* Vol. 30, November 1901, p. 525.

36. Helman, Harley H. *Church of the Brethren in Southern Ohio*. Elgin, Illinois: Brethren Publishing House, 1955. p. 507.

37. *Brethren Family Almanac*, 1903. Inside cover.

38. Photo loaned by Orpha Book, North Manchester, Indiana.

39. Property of the family of the author.

40. Photo loaned by Alda Garber, Harrisonburg, Virginia.

41. Property of Elmer Bowman, Hagerstown, Indiana.

42. Photo loaned by Alma Wise, Onekama, Michigan.

43. Photo loaned by Pauline Geyer Kagarice, Huntingdon, Pennsylvania.

44. Property of the family of the author.

45. Property of Georgeanna Lorenz, Greentown, Indiana.

46. Gift to the author by Aaron S. Hollinger, Elizabethtown, Pennsylvania.

47. Nead. *Theological Writings*, p. 72.

48. Helman. *History of Southern Ohio*, p. 561.

49. Photo by the author.

50. Swatches gift to the author by Martin's

Store, Elizabethtown, Pennsylvania.

51. Property of the family of the author.

52. Gift to the author by Martin's Store, Elizabethtown, Pennsylvania.

53. Ibid.

54. Photo from the family collection of the author.

55. Property of the family of the author.

56. Pyle, Howard. "A Peculiar People." *Harper's New Monthly Magazine*, Vol. 79, October 1889, p. 780.

57. Photo loaned by Anna Ober Gibble, Manheim, Pennsylvania.

58. Photo from the family collection of the author.

59. Lloyd, *Scribner's Magazine.* Vol. 30 November 1901, p. 523.

60. Emmert, David. *Reminiscences of Juniata College, 1876-1901.* Illustrated and published by the author, Huntingdon, Pennsylvania, 1901. p. 114.

61. Photo loaned by Frank Replogle, West Lafayette, Indiana.

62. Photo from the family collection of the author.

63. Ibid.

64. Property of the family of the author.

65. Photo loaned by Linda Fike, Uniontown, Pennsylvania.

66. Photo by the author.

67. Property of the family of the author.

68. Photo from the family collection of the author.

69. Ibid.

70. Ibid.

71. Photo by the author.

72. Property of the family of the author.

73. Property of Georgeanna Lorenz, Greentown, Indiana.

74. Ibid.

75. Senger, Nettie M. *House of Sanger, History of the Descendents of Conrad Sanger, Son of John Senger.* Nashville, Tennessee: Ambrose Printing Company, 1956. p. 102.

76. Photo from the family collection of the author.

77. Nead. Theological Writings, p. 134.

78. Photo loaned by Kathren Holsopple, LaVerne, California.

79. Photo loaned by Esther Austin, Bloomington, Indiana.

80. Property of Mary Kay Rinehart, Hagerstown, Indiana.

81. Howard, Clifford. "A Peace Loving People." *The Ladies Home Journal.* Vol. 15, July 1898, p. 5.

82. Photo loaned by Sarah Spitler,

Bringhurst, Indiana.

83. Property of Della Hoover Nicholson, Hagerstown, Indiana.

84. Photo loaned by Linda Fike, Uniontown, Pennsylvania.

85. Property of Margaret Paul, Mooreland, Indiana.

86. Property of Grace Madeira Shuler, Huntingdon, Pennsylvania.

87. Property of the First Church of the Brethren, Philadelphia, Pennsylvania.

88. Photo secured from Allied Pix Service, Harrisburg, Pennsylvania.

89. Photo by Don Honick, Church of the Brethren General Offices, Elgin, Illinois.

90. Photo by the author.

91. Property of LaVona Meyers Hildreth, Lafayette, Indiana.

92. Property of Anna Bashor Keeney, Bethel, Pennsylvania.

93. Property of Ella Carper, Palmyra, Pennsylvania.

94. Ibid.

95. Property of Wilbur Royer, Portsmouth, Ohio.

96. Property of Mary Lamb, Hagerstown, Indiana.

97. Property of Goldie Reed Rohrer, Plymouth, Indiana.

98. Property of Mary Lamb, Hagerstown, Indiana.

99. Property of Alta Hilbert, Hagerstown, Indiana.

100. Property of Mary Lamb, Hagerstown, Indiana.

101. Photo loaned by Kathren Royer Holsopple, LaVerne, California.

102. Photo by the author.

103. Property of Elizabethtown Church of the Brethren, Elizabethtown, Pennsylvania.

104. Photo by the author.

105. Photo by Don Honick, Church of the Brethren General Offices, Elgin, Illinois.

106. *The Inglenook*, Vol. 8, August 21, 1906, p. 818.

107. Available at Hager's Store, Lancaster, Pennsylvania; and Marian and Ruth Shop, Mount Joy, Pennsylvania, 1968.

108. Ibid.

109. Ibid.

110. Property of the family of the author.

111. Ibid.

112. Property of Goldie Reed Rohrer, Plymouth, Indiana.

113. Property of Martha Wise, Spiceland, Indiana.

114. Made for the author by Katie Long Enders, Plymouth, Indiana.

115. Nead. *Theological Writings.* p. 134.

116. Photo loaned by Kathren Royer Holsopple, LaVerne, California.

117. Photo loaned by Iva Glunt, Richmond, Indiana.

118. Photo loaned by Kathren Holsopple, LaVerne, California.

119. Photo loaned by George Hildreth, Lafayette, Indiana.

120. Photo loaned by Iva Glunt, Richmond, Indiana.

121. Photo from the family collection of the author.

122. Property of Georgeanna Lorenz, Greentown, Indiana.

123. Property of Iva Glunt, Richmond, Indiana.

124. Property of the family of the author.

125. Property of Georgeanna Lorenz, Greentown, Indiana.

126. Photo from the family collection of the author.

127. Ibid.

128. Photo loaned by Florence Hufford Replogle, West Lafayette, Indiana.

129. Photo from the family collection of the author.

130. Property of Georgeanna Lorenz, Greentown, Indiana.

131. Ibid.

132. Photo loaned by Marianne Kruegar Michael, Iowa City, Iowa.

133. Photo loaned by Mary Hay Rinehart, Hagerstown, Indiana

134. Photo loaned by Esther Heisler, Freeport, Michigan.

135. Property of Grace Madeira Shuler, Huntingdon, Pennsylvania.

136. Property of Helen Synder Davis, Lansdale, Pennsylvania.

137. Supplied by Barbara Longnecker, Neffsville, Pennsylvania.

138. Photo loaned by Marianne Kruegar Michael, Iowa City, Iowa.

139. Photo from the family collection of the author.

140. Photo loaned by Iva Glunt, Richmond, Indiana.

141. Photo loaned by Martha Shively Wise, Spiceland, Indiana.

142. Property of Goldie Reed Rohrer, Plymouth, Indiana.

143. Senger. *House of Sanger.* p. 21.

144. Photo loaned by Mary Ellen Steele Vaughn, South Bend, Indiana.

145. Photo loaned by Barbara Longenecker, Neffsville, Pennsylvania.

146. Property of Iva Glunt, Richmond, Indiana.

147. Photo property of the Elizabethtown

Church of the Brethren, Elizabethtown, Pennsylvania.

148. Property of Helen Snyder Davis, Lansdale, Pennsylvania.

149. Photo by the author.

150. Photo from the family collection of the author.

151. Property of Iva Glunt, Richmond, Indiana.

152. Ibid.

153. Property of LaVona Meyers Hildreth, Lafayette, Indiana.

154. Property of Marianne Kruegar Michael, Iowa City, Iowa.

155. Property of Georgeanna Lorenz, Greentown, Indiana.

156. Property of Martha Shively Wise, Spiceland, Indiana.

157. Property of Minnie Wampole, Greens Fork, Indiana.

158. Property of Clarence Stout, Hagerstown, Indiana.

159. Property of the family of the author.

160. Property of the late Olyve Wyles, Martinsburg, Pennsylvania.

161. Property of the family of the author.

162. Photo loaned by Anna Ober Gibble, Manheim, Pennsylvania.

163. Photo loaned by Marianne Kruegar

Michael, Iowa City, Iowa.

164. Gift to the author by Mary L. Vance Riethof, Lafayette Hill, Pennsylvania.

165. Photo from the family collection of the author.

166. Property of Iva Glunt, Richmond, Indiana.

167. Property of Helen Synder Davis, Lansdale, Pennsylvania.

168. Property of Georgeanna Lorenz, Greentown, Indiana.

169. Property of the family of the author.

170. Property of Georgeanna Lorenz, Greentown, Indiana.

171. Ibid.

172. Property of Edith Rohrer Rupel, West Lafayette, Indiana.

173. Property of the family of the author.

174. Property of Edith Rohrer Rupel, West Lafayette, Indiana.

175. Ibid.

176. Property of Marianne Kruegar Michael, Iowa City, Iowa.

177. Photo from the family collection of the author.

178. Property of Edith Rohrer Rupel, West Lafayette, Indiana.

179. Photo loaned by Kathren Royer Holsopple, LaVerne, California.

180. Photo loaned by Juniata College, Huntingdon, Pennsylvania.

181. Photo loaned by Grant Steele. Walkerton, Indiana.

182. Photo loaned by Juniata College, Huntingdon, Pennsylvania.

183. Photo from the family collection of the author.

184. Photo loaned by Kathren Royer Holsopple, LaVerne, California.

185. Photo from the family collection of the author.

186. Photo by Lois Rupel Tuinstra, Eugene, Oregon.

187. Photo loaned by Ethel Harshbarger Henderson, Huntingdon, Pennsylvania.

188. Ibid.

189. Ibid.

190. Photo loaned by Orpha Book, North Manchester, Indiana.

191. Photo loaned by Kathren Royer Holsopple, LaVerne, California.

192. Photo loaned by Lewis Emmert Huntingdon, Pennsylvania.

193. Photo from the family collection of the author.

194. Ibid.

195. Photo loaned by Grace Madeira Shuler, Huntingdon, Pennsylvania.

196. Photo loaned by Frank Replogle, West Lafayette, Indiana.

197. Photo loaned by Anna Ober Gibble, Manheim, Pennsylvania.

198. Photo by Lois Rupel Tuinstra, Eugene, Oregon.

199. Photo by the author.

200. Nead. *Theological Writings*. p. 126.

201. Photo a gift to the author by Alma Van Winkle, North Manchester, Indiana.

202. Photo from the family collection of the author.

203. Photo loaned by Kathren Royer Holsopple, LaVerne, California.

204. Photo from the family collection of the author.

205. Photo loaned by Frank Replogle, West Lafayette, Indiana.

206. Photo loaned by Gay Steiner, Russiaville, Indiana.

207. Photo by Lloyd S. Jones. *The Youngstown Vindicator*, Rotogravure Section, January 24, 1971.

208. Photo from the family collection of the author.

209. Photo loaned by Alda Garber, Harrisonburg, Virginia.

210. Property of Lois Rupel Tuinstra, Eugene, Oregon.

211. Photo by Don Honick, Church of the Brethren General Offices, Elgin, Illinois.

APPENDIX B

Distribution of Annual Meeting Minutes on Dress

Table 1. Distribution of Annual Meeting Minutes Prescribing Items of Clothing and Polity of the Church of the Brethren, 1800-1928.

Year	1800	01	02	03	04	05	06	07	08	09	10	11	12	13	14	15	16	17	18	19	20	21	22	23	24	25	26	27	28	29	30	31	32	33	34
Fashionable Dress																																			
In General	–	–	–	–	9*	–	–	–	–	–	–	–	–	–	–	–	–	2	–	5	–	–	8	–	–	–	–	–	–	–	–	–	–	–	9
Item of Clothing																																			
For a Brother																																			
Hair & Beard	–	–	–	–	5	–	–	–	–	–	–	–	–	–	–	–	–	–	–	–	–	–	1	–	–	–	–	–	–	–	–	–	–	–	–
Hat	–	–	–	–	–	–	–	–	–	–	–	–	–	–	–	–	–	–	–	–	–	–	–	–	–	–	–	–	–	–	–	–	–	–	–
Coat	–	–	–	–	–	–	–	–	–	–	–	–	–	–	–	–	–	–	–	–	–	–	–	–	–	–	–	–	–	–	–	–	–	–	–
Necktie	–	–	–	–	–	–	–	–	–	–	–	–	–	–	–	–	–	–	–	–	–	–	–	–	–	–	–	–	–	–	–	–	–	–	–
Other	–	–	–	–	–	–	–	–	–	–	–	–	–	–	–	–	–	–	–	–	–	–	–	–	–	–	–	–	–	–	–	–	–	–	–
For a Sister																																			
Hair	–	–	–	–	–	–	–	–	–	–	–	–	–	–	–	–	–	–	–	–	–	–	–	–	–	–	–	–	–	–	–	–	–	–	–
Cap	–	–	–	–	–	–	–	–	–	–	–	–	–	–	–	–	–	–	–	–	–	–	–	–	–	–	–	–	–	–	–	–	–	–	–
Bonnet	–	–	–	–	–	–	–	–	–	–	–	–	–	–	–	–	–	–	–	–	–	–	–	–	–	–	–	–	–	–	–	–	–	–	–
Dress	–	–	–	–	–	–	–	–	–	–	–	–	–	–	–	–	–	–	–	–	–	–	–	–	–	–	–	–	–	–	–	–	–	–	–
Other	–	–	–	–	–	–	–	–	–	–	–	–	–	–	–	–	–	–	–	–	–	–	–	–	–	–	–	–	–	–	–	–	–	–	–
Gold	–	–	–	–	–	–	–	–	–	–	–	–	–	–	–	–	–	–	–	–	–	–	–	–	–	–	–	–	–	–	–	–	–	–	–
Church Polity																																			
Authority	–	–	–	–	–	–	–	–	–	–	–	–	–	–	–	–	–	–	–	–	–	–	–	–	–	–	–	–	–	–	–	–	–	–	–
Baptism	–	–	–	–	–	–	–	–	–	–	–	–	–	–	–	–	–	–	–	–	–	–	–	–	–	–	–	–	–	–	–	–	–	–	–
Letter	–	–	–	–	–	–	–	–	–	–	–	–	–	–	–	–	–	–	–	–	–	–	–	–	–	–	–	–	–	–	–	–	–	–	–
Lay Member	–	–	–	–	–	–	–	–	–	–	–	–	–	–	–	–	–	–	–	–	–	–	–	–	–	–	–	–	–	–	–	–	–	–	–
Officiant	–	–	–	–	–	–	–	–	–	–	–	–	–	–	–	–	–	–	–	–	–	–	–	–	–	–	–	–	–	–	–	–	–	–	–
Congregation	–	–	–	–	–	–	–	–	–	–	–	–	–	–	–	–	–	–	–	–	–	–	–	–	–	–	–	–	–	–	–	–	–	–	–
Dress Reform																																			
Committee	–	–	–	–	–	–	–	–	–	–	–	–	–	–	–	–	–	–	–	–	–	–	–	–	–	–	–	–	–	–	–	–	–	–	–

* Number of Article in Minutes.

Table 1. Continued

Year	1800 35	36	37	38	39	40	41	42	43	44	45	46	47	48	49	50	51	52	53	54	55	56	57	58	59	60	61	62	63	64	65	66
Fashionable Dress																																
In General	–	–	–	–	–	7	–	–	–	–	6	10	–	–	–	–	–	–	–	–	–	–	–	6	–	–	–	22,34,63	–	8	–	27,47
Item of Clothing																																
For a Brother																																
Hair & Beard	–	–	–	–	–	–	–	–	–	–	–	11	–	–	–	–	–	–	7	19	–	–	–	–	–	–	–	12	–	8	–	27,47
Hat	–	–	–	–	–	–	–	–	–	–	–	–	–	–	3	–	–	–	–	–	–	–	–	–	–	–	–	–	–	–	–	–
Coat	–	–	–	–	–	–	–	–	–	–	–	–	9	–	–	–	–	–	–	–	–	–	–	–	–	–	–	–	–	–	–	27
Necktie	–	–	–	–	–	–	–	–	–	–	–	–	–	–	–	–	–	–	–	–	–	–	–	–	–	–	–	–	–	–	–	–
Other	–	–	–	–	–	–	–	–	–	–	–	–	–	–	–	–	–	–	–	–	–	–	–	–	–	–	–	–	–	10	–	–
For a Sister																																
Hair	–	–	–	–	–	–	–	–	–	–	–	–	–	–	–	–	–	–	–	–	–	–	–	–	–	–	–	–	–	–	–	–
Cap	–	–	–	–	–	–	–	–	–	–	–	–	–	6	–	–	–	–	–	–	–	26	–	–	–	–	3	19	–	–	–	27
Bonnet	–	–	–	–	–	–	–	–	–	–	–	–	–	–	3	–	–	–	–	–	–	–	–	–	–	–	3	–	–	–	–	27
Dress	–	–	–	–	–	–	–	–	–	–	–	–	–	–	–	–	–	–	–	–	–	–	–	–	–	–	–	22,34	3	–	–	27
Other	–	–	–	–	–	–	–	–	–	–	–	–	–	–	–	–	–	–	–	–	–	–	–	–	–	–	–	–	–	–	–	–
Gold	–	–	–	–	–	–	–	–	–	–	–	–	–	–	–	–	–	–	–	8	–	–	10	56	–	–	–	–	–	7	–	27
Church Polity																																
Authority	–	–	–	–	–	–	–	–	–	–	–	–	–	–	–	–	–	–	–	–	–	–	–	–	–	–	–	–	–	–	–	–
Baptism	–	8	–	–	–	–	–	–	–	–	–	–	–	–	–	–	–	–	–	–	–	–	–	–	–	–	–	63	–	–	–	–
Letter	–	–	–	–	–	–	–	–	–	–	–	–	–	–	–	–	–	–	–	–	–	–	–	–	–	–	–	–	–	–	–	–
Lay Member	–	–	–	–	–	–	–	–	–	–	–	11	–	–	25	–	–	–	–	–	–	–	–	6	–	–	3	38	–	–	–	27
Officiant	–	–	–	–	–	–	–	–	–	–	–	–	–	–	–	–	–	–	–	19	–	–	–	–	–	–	–	–	8	–	–	26
Congregation	–	–	–	–	–	–	–	–	–	–	–	–	–	–	–	–	–	–	–	–	–	–	–	–	–	–	–	–	–	–	–	–
Dress Reform Committee	–	–	–	–	–	–	–	–	–	–	–	–	–	–	–	–	–	–	–	–	–	–	–	–	–	–	–	–	–	–	–	–

181

Table 1. Continued

182

	1800																												
Year	67	68	69	70	71	72	73	74	75	76	77	78	79	80	81	82	83	84	85	86	87	88	89	90	91	92	93	94	95
Fashionable Dress																													
In General	4	–	–	33	–	–	–	–	–	27	–	–	–	16	10	–	–	–	–	2	–	–	–	–	–	–	–	–	–
Item of Clothing																													
For a Brother																													
Hair & Beard	4	20	14	–	–	–	–	5	–	–	–	14	–	–	–	2,3	–	–	–	2	–	2,3	–	–	–	–	4,5	–	–
Hat	–	–	22	–	–	–	–	–	–	–	–	–	–	–	–	–	–	–	–	–	9	12	–	–	–	–	–	–	–
Coat	–	–	–	–	–	–	–	–	–	11	9	–	–	–	–	–	–	–	–	–	–	–	–	–	–	–	4,9	–	–
Necktie	–	–	–	–	–	–	–	–	–	–	–	–	–	–	–	–	–	–	–	–	–	–	–	–	–	–	–	–	–
Other	–	–	–	–	–	–	–	–	–	–	–	–	–	–	–	–	–	–	–	–	–	–	4	–	–	–	–	–	–
For a Sister																													
Hair	–	–	–	–	–	–	–	–	–	–	–	–	–	–	–	–	–	–	–	–	–	–	–	–	–	–	–	–	–
Cap	–	–	22	–	–	–	–	–	–	–	–	5	–	–	–	–	–	–	–	2,12	–	–	–	–	–	–	11	–	–
Bonnet	–	–	–	–	–	–	–	–	–	21	16	–	–	14	21	–	–	–	–	2	–	–	–	–	–	–	–	–	–
Dress	–	–	–	–	–	–	–	–	–	–	–	–	–	–	–	–	–	–	–	12	–	–	–	–	–	–	–	–	–
Other	–	–	–	–	–	–	–	–	–	–	–	–	–	–	19	–	–	–	–	–	–	–	1,4	–	–	–	–	–	–
Gold	–	–	–	–	–	–	–	–	–	–	–	–	–	–	–	–	–	–	–	2	–	–	2	–	19½	–	–	–	–
Church Polity																													
Authority	–	–	18	–	–	–	–	–	–	–	–	–	–	–	–	–	–	–	–	–	–	–	–	–	–	–	–	–	–
Baptism	–	–	–	–	–	–	–	–	–	–	–	–	–	–	–	–	–	–	–	7	–	–	–	–	–	–	–	–	–
Letter	–	–	–	–	–	–	–	–	–	–	–	5	–	–	1	–	–	–	–	2	–	–	–	–	5	–	–	–	–
Lay Member	19	–	–	22	–	–	–	–	–	–	–	–	–	–	–	–	–	–	–	–	–	–	–	–	–	–	–	–	–
Officiant	–	–	21	27	3	–	18	–	–	8	1,31	5,14	–	–	1,10,15,16,17	18	–	–	–	3,6	–	–	6	6	–	–	12	7	–
Congregation	–	–	–	33	–	–	–	–	–	27	–	–	–	–	–	–	–	–	–	6	–	–	–	–	–	R**	–	–	–
Dress Reform																													
Committee	–	–	–	–	–	–	–	–	–	–	–	–	–	–	–	–	–	–	–	–	–	–	–	–	–	–	–	–	–

** Committee Report

Table 1. Continued

	96	97	98	99	00 (1900)	01	02	03	04	05	06	07	08	09	10	11	12	13	14	15	16	17	18	19	20	21	22	23	24	25	26	27	28
Year																																	
Fashionable Dress																																	
In General	–	–	3	–	–	–	–	–	–	–	–	–	–	5	R	R	6	–	4	3	–	6	4	8	9	4	5	6	–	–	R	–	–
Item of Clothing																																	
For a Brother																																	
Hair & Beard	–	–	–	–	3	–	–	–	–	–	–	–	–	–	–	R	–	–	–	–	–	R	–	–	–	–	–	6	–	11	–	–	–
Hat	–	3	–	–	–	–	–	–	–	–	–	–	–	–	–	–	–	–	–	–	–	–	–	–	–	–	–	–	–	–	–	–	–
Coat	–	–	–	–	3	–	–	–	–	–	–	–	–	–	–	R	–	–	4	5	–	R	–	–	9	–	–	–	–	–	–	–	–
Necktie	–	3	–	–	7	–	–	–	–	–	–	–	–	–	–	–	–	–	–	–	–	–	–	–	9	–	–	–	–	–	–	–	–
Other	–	–	10	–	13	–	–	9	–	–	–	–	–	–	–	R	–	–	–	–	–	R	–	–	–	–	–	–	–	–	–	–	–
For a Sister																																	
Hair	–	–	–	–	–	–	–	–	–	–	–	–	–	–	–	–	–	–	–	–	–	–	–	–	–	–	–	–	–	–	R	–	–
Cap	–	3	–	–	–	–	–	–	–	–	–	–	–	–	–	R	–	–	–	–	–	R	–	–	–	–	6	6	–	6	R	–	–
Bonnet	3	3	–	–	1	–	–	–	–	–	3	–	–	–	–	R	–	–	–	–	–	R	–	–	9	6	–	–	–	–	–	–	–
Dress	–	3	–	–	–	–	–	–	–	–	–	–	–	–	–	R	–	–	–	–	–	R	–	–	–	–	–	–	–	–	–	–	–
Other	–	–	–	–	–	–	–	–	–	–	–	–	–	–	–	R	–	–	–	–	–	R	–	–	–	–	–	–	–	–	–	–	–
Gold	14	–	–	–	3	–	–	–	–	–	1	–	–	–	–	R	–	–	–	–	–	R	–	–	9	–	–	–	–	–	R	–	–
Church Polity																																	
Authority	–	–	–	–	–	–	–	–	–	–	–	–	–	–	–	–	–	–	–	–	–	–	–	–	–	–	–	–	–	–	–	–	–
Baptism	–	–	–	–	–	–	–	–	–	–	–	–	–	–	–	–	–	–	–	–	–	–	–	–	–	–	–	–	–	–	–	–	–
Letter	–	–	–	–	–	–	–	–	–	–	–	–	–	–	–	–	–	–	3	–	2	–	–	–	–	6	–	7	5	–	R	R	–
Lay Member	–	3	–	–	–	–	–	–	–	–	–	–	–	–	–	R	–	–	–	–	–	R	–	–	–	–	–	–	–	–	R	R	–
Officiant	R	–	3	–	8	–	–	–	–	–	–	–	–	–	–	R	–	–	–	–	–	R	4	–	–	–	–	–	–	–	R	–	–
Congregation	–	–	–	–	–	–	–	–	–	–	3	–	–	–	–	–	–	–	–	–	–	–	–	–	–	–	–	–	–	–	–	–	–
Dress Reform Committee	–	–	–	–	–	–	–	–	–	–	–	–	–	–	10	R	R	R	R	R	R	R	R	R	R	R	R	R	R,3R	R	R	R	–